Fueling the Online Trade Revolution

A New Customs Security Framework to Secure and Facilitate Small Business E-commerce

PROJECT CODIRECTORS
Heather A. Conley
Kati Suominen

AUTHOR
Kati Suominen

A Report of the CSIS Europe Program

April 2015

CSIS | CENTER FOR STRATEGIC & INTERNATIONAL STUDIES

ROWMAN & LITTLEFIELD
Lanham • Boulder • New York • London

About CSIS

For over 50 years, the Center for Strategic and International Studies (CSIS) has worked to develop solutions to the world's greatest policy challenges. Today, CSIS scholars are providing strategic insights and bipartisan policy solutions to help decisionmakers chart a course toward a better world.

CSIS is a nonprofit organization headquartered in Washington, D.C. The Center's 220 full-time staff and large network of affiliated scholars conduct research and analysis and develop policy initiatives that look into the future and anticipate change.

Founded at the height of the Cold War by David M. Abshire and Admiral Arleigh Burke, CSIS was dedicated to finding ways to sustain American prominence and prosperity as a force for good in the world. Since 1962, CSIS has become one of the world's preeminent international institutions focused on defense and security; regional stability; and transnational challenges ranging from energy and climate to global health and economic integration.

Former U.S. senator Sam Nunn has chaired the CSIS Board of Trustees since 1999. Former deputy secretary of defense John J. Hamre became the Center's president and chief executive officer in 2000.

CSIS does not take specific policy positions; accordingly, all views expressed herein should be understood to be solely those of the author(s).

Acknowledgments

This report was made possible by the generous support of eBay Inc. The author would also like to thank all participants in the expert roundtable discussion carried out in the preparation of this report; Vivian Jones, James McGowan, and Marianne Rowden for subsequent comments; and Heather Conley and James Mina at CSIS for outstanding collaboration.

ISBN: 978-1-4422-4090-2 (pb); 978-1-4422-4091-9 (eBook)

Center for Strategic & International Studies
1616 Rhode Island Avenue, NW
Washington, DC 20036
202-887-0200 | www.csis.org

Rowman & Littlefield
4501 Forbes Boulevard
Lanham, MD 20706
301-459-3366 | www.rowman.com

Contents

1 Introduction

Across the United States, individuals and small businesses are increasingly buying and selling goods and services online. According to U.S. Census Bureau, the total number of online transactions in the United States grew from $3 trillion in 2006 to $5.4 trillion in 2012, to about a third of U.S. GDP. Increasingly, these transactions are cross border. By 2017, a third of U.S. business-to-consumer (B2C) and consumer-to-consumer (C2C) e-commerce transactions will be with foreign counterparts, up from 16 percent today.[1]

Behind these trends are the previously marginal participants in trade—American small businesses, entrepreneurs, and consumers that transact with foreign buyers and sellers online. E-commerce is propitious for these players: it drastically lowers the costs for buyers and sellers located far apart to gain visibility and transact with each other. In addition, as hundreds of millions of individual consumers around the world leverage their laptops, tablets, and phones to buy goods and services online, companies of all sizes even in the most distant parts of the world are more likely to be discovered and turned into exporters.

The U.S. and global e-commerce marketplace is only in its infancy. According to projections, online trade in the transatlantic market is expected to grow 10 to 14 percent annually, well above the expected overall global trade growth of 6 to 8 percent per annum, to exceed $370 billion in the United States by 2017. The Asia-Pacific region will see explosive growth as well, with its e-commerce marketplace soaring to $450 billion by 2017.[2] B2C and C2C transactions are poised to expand further as 4 billion to-be Internet users log on across the developing world in the coming two decades. These trends are reshaping the traditional patterns in world trade, which is overwhelmingly driven by large corporations, and of which 90 percent is business-to-business (B2B), often intrafirm trade among multinational company branches.

The online revolution holds extraordinary potential for expanding U.S. small business exports and entrepreneurship. E-commerce enables a large number of U.S. small

1. Paypal, "Modern Spice Routes: The Cultural Impact and Economic Opportunity of Cross-Border Shopping," 2013, https://www.paypal-media.com/assets/pdf/fact_sheet/PayPal_ModernSpiceRoutes_Report_Final.pdf. For an excellent study of e-commerce in the United States, see U.S. International Trade Commission (USITC), Digital Trade in the U.S. and Global Economies, Part 1 (Washington, DC: USITC, July 2013), http://www.usitc.gov/publications/332/pub4415.pdf.
2. ChannelAdvisor, "Sharpen Your Cross-Border Trade Strategy: Explore Each Market," n.d., http://www.channeladvisor.com/platform/cross-border-trade/.

companies and entrepreneurs to export, diversify their markets, scale their sales, and expand their businesses at relatively low cost. It also gives U.S. consumers access to a wider variety of products and services at lower cost, making all Americans better off. In addition, enhancing companies' productivity and lowering international trade costs, e-commerce also accelerates economic growth and job creation in the United States.

At the same time, the rise of e-commerce is creating pressing policy questions, such as how to align customs security frameworks with the future of trade. How should policy makers revise custom security frameworks when millions of businesses and individuals around the world increasingly engage in billions of microtransactions, often resulting in shipments of small parcels from small businesses to individual consumers? The purpose of this report is to answer these questions.

So far, customs security regimes around the world have been tailored to the patterns of traditional trade: large trade volumes shipped by large and midsize companies with staff trained to comply with trade rules. Customs regimes are not optimally designed for trade between small enterprises and consumers, players with limited trade compliance capabilities. While the U.S. government and governments around the world have fashioned so-called trusted trader and authorized economic operator (AEO) programs to streamline trade compliance and fast-track low-risk companies' trade, these programs' criteria are extremely challenging for small businesses to meet, let alone for individuals as importers of record. This problem also affects large companies, given that many of them now sell online to individuals and small businesses. There, in short, is a mismatch between today's customs security regimes and tomorrow's trade.

Refashioning customs security regimes to accommodate the online revolution is not easy. It involves complex trade-offs between facilitating and securing trade. Governments have legitimate security concerns related to the fact that world trade is diffuse—increasingly driven by countless small players shipping small parcels. A particular concern in the future might be that governments become wary of these small entrants in trade and exercise excessive scrutiny over them, thereby undermining a new and promising area of international trade. Yet a hands-off approach may also not work: even a few security incidents could incite a regulatory crackdown that decelerates or altogether deters legitimate small business trade.

As online, consumer-driven trade expands, there is a need for fresh policy thinking on regulatory frameworks and procedures that would secure trade without sacrificing the opportunity for small businesses to engage in trade and reach overseas customers in a timely and cost-effective fashion. This report puts forth a set of ideas that would align the U.S. customs security regime with the future of trade. The report seeks to answer the following questions:

- What is the state of trade facilitation and customs security regimes in the United States and abroad? What are the key criteria that importers and exporters need to meet in order for their goods to cross borders?

- What are the major requirements for U.S. companies that are seeking to fast-track their cross-border shipments while satisfying security and customs requirements? What kinds of companies are able to meet these criteria, and what are their incentives? To what extent have these programs been multilateralized?
- What do future importers and exporters look like? How are online buyers and sellers different from the traditional, brick-and-mortar offline buyers and sellers, and how are they changing world trade? How do they currently comply with trade regulations, and what are their capabilities and incentives to enter customs security programs that fast-track trade?
- What is the future of risk in trade? How does the rise of online trade alter the security landscape in trade, and what should customs be prepared for?
- What does an ideal future customs security framework look like—one that secures trade while at the same time facilitating millions of cross-border transactions, helping millions of small businesses and individuals to engage in and profit from trade? What should the U.S. customs security framework look like, and how could it be multilateralized?

This report is organized as follows. The following section reviews existing security regimes and their functioning in the United States. Section three focuses on online sellers and buyers, contrasting them with their brick-and-mortar offline counterparts. The fourth section puts forth a set of ideas on structuring customs regimes so as to secure and facilitate online trade. Section five concludes.

2 Customs Security Regimes: Where Are We?

After 9/11, the United States and other countries revised customs and port security measures to combat terrorism, in many ways by pushing U.S. borders out. There have been three broad sets of reforms.

The first set includes the Container Security Initiative (CSI) founded in January 2002 to address maritime cargo. Under CSI, U.S. Customs and Border Protection (CBP) secures U.S-bound containers in foreign ports before the containers are placed on vessels coming to the United States. CSI is now operational at 58 ports in North America, Europe, Asia, Africa, the Middle East, and Latin America.

In addition to CSI, the CBP uses a predictive analytics system called the Automated Targeting System (ATS) and other strategic intelligence methods to prevent weapons of mass destruction, drugs, or other contraband entering the United States in a container. CBP also scans higher-risk containers using nonintrusive inspection (NII) technologies, including large-scale X-ray and gamma ray machines and radiation detection devices, and it may also carry out physical inspections at any time during the entry process.[1]

The CSI elevated the filing requirements on shippers and importers. The "24-hour Manifest Rule" announced in late 2002 requires carriers to electronically file their cargo manifests with the CBP 24 hours prior to loading a foreign port for the United States. Table 1 shows the U.S. import process.

The 24-hour rule succeeded at collecting and transmitting import data. However, the data was often inconsistent. In response, in 2009 CBP announced the second major reform to the U.S customs regime: the Importer Security Filing (ISF), or the "10 + 2" rule, as defined in the SAFE Port Act. The new rule, pertinent to maritime cargo, made the U.S. importer (or the importer's broker or freight forwarder) responsible for providing granular data on the cargo at least 24 hours prior to its arrival at a U.S. port. 10 + 2 refers to the 10 data elements

1. ATS is a web-based enforcement tool. CBP weighs the risk indicators and classifies the weighted risk scores as low, medium, or high risk. CPB officers are generally required to review shipment data for all medium-risk and high-risk shipments and hold high-risk shipments for examination.

Table 1. U.S. Import Process

Pre-Entry	*Entry*	*Post-Entry*
• Importers and countries provide advance electronic cargo information • Data are screened through Automated Targeting System • Containers may be subject to nonintrusive inspection, import scanning, and/or inspection at foreign port or U.S. port	• Importers file entry documents within 15 days of cargo's arrival at point of entry • Containers may be subject to additional scanning and inspection • CPB officers make a preliminary determination on admissibility • Importers may submit additional evidence to prove admissibility as necessary • Admissible cargo is released; importers must file entry summary documents with additional customs data • CBP uses entry summary documents to make an initial assessment of duties owed	• Importer has up to one year to challenge assessment unless liquidation period is extended • Entry is liquidated, resulting in final assessment of duties or drawback entries • CPB may audit importers as part of trade enforcement investigations

Data source: Vivian C. Jones and Marc R. Rosenblum, "U.S. Customs and Border Protection: Trade Facilitation, Enforcement, and Security," Congressional Research Service, March 22, 2013.

importers need to provide and the 2 data elements the carrier is required to file. The following 10 data elements are required from the importer:[2]

- Manufacturer (or supplier) name and address
- Seller (or owner) name and address
- Buyer (or owner) name and address
- Ship-to name and address
- Container stuffing location
- Consolidator (stuffer) name and address
- Importer of record number/foreign trade zone applicant identification number
- Consignee number(s)

2. When filing the 10 + 2 data, importers utilize a software to
    - Access trading partners and view/edit their information
    - Load data from electronic files or allow for manual entry of data
    - Notify users automatically when work needs to be completed for filing purposes
    - Connect to CBP, allowing the importer to file the ISF
    - Validate classification data for all filings before transmitting to CBP
    - Designate fields to automatically populate with consistent data across all filings for a company
    - Track the events of a shipment and coinciding ISF data elements triggered by those events

- Country of origin
- Commodity Harmonized Tariff Schedule number to six digits

The carrier is required to fill two data elements:

- Vessel stow plan
- Container status messages

The third major reform to the post-9/11 customs security regime aimed to combine security and trade facilitation, a critical goal in a world of just-in-time production and complex supply chains. It formed part of a global wave of security reforms: governments around the world created automated economic operator (AEO) and "trusted trader" programs for low-risk companies to become eligible for expedited customs processing. These programs align with standards set forth in the World Customs Organization (WCO) Standards to Secure and Facilitate Global Trade (SAFE Framework) focused on supply chain security.

The U.S. equivalent to an AEO is the Customs-Trade Partnership against Terrorism (C-TPAT). First launched in November 2001, C-TPAT requires companies to enter into an "anti-terror partnership" with the government and agree to work with CBP to protect the supply chain, identify security gaps, and implement specific security measures and best practices, in exchange for improved trade facilitation such as a lower ATS score. Initially for importers, in September 2014, CBP extended C-TPAT also for exporters.

C-TPAT primarily focuses on securing supply chains.[3] Its affiliate program, Importer Self-Assessment (ISA), focuses on strengthening companies' internal controls in order to comply with customs laws and regulations. Only C-TPAT participants can be part of ISA. In June 2014, CBP rolled out a Trusted Trader Program test that will combine C-TPAT and ISA and run for 18 months. It is implemented in collaboration with the U.S. Consumer Product Safety Commission and the U.S. Food and Drug Administration. Combining security and compliance, it aligns with the AEO programs around the world. There initially are fewer than 10 company participants.

Challenges in Securing and Facilitating Trade

The reforms to the customs security regime have had a mixed record. There are three broad challenges in particular: (1) Securing vs. facilitating trade; (2) low C-TPAT uptake; and (3) challenges of mutual recognition.

3. A C-TPAT-related program, Free and Secure Trade System (FAST), fast-tracks commercial truck drivers who have completed background checks and fulfilled eligibility requirements and whose imports have supply chains that are fully C-TPAT certified.

SECURING VS. FACILITATING TRADE

The first challenge is reaching the balance between securing and facilitating trade. While CBP is mandated to scan 100 percent of incoming cargo, and all containers are subject to targeted risk assessment and radiation scanning, overall some 25 percent of containers entering the United States by all modes of transportation were subject to secondary scanning and inspection (i.e., NII and physical inspection, or both).[4] In FY 2011, as many as 89 percent of containerized imports entering by rail were scanned and/or inspected, but only 27 percent of imports entering by truck and 4 percent entering by sea were scanned by NII and/or physically inspected.[5]

Two opposing views have emerged on how the government should address the low scanning rates. The first argues that the U.S. inspection system should be more risk-averse—that CBP should place more emphasis on securing cargo, even if that costs more and causes delays. The other side argues that the economic cost of inspections is already too high. For example, according to Bloomberg, delays at the U.S.-Mexico border amounted to almost $7.8 billion in lost economic output in 2011, and the cost will rise to $14.7 billion if the value of U.S.-Mexico truck trade reaches the forecast level, $463 billion, by 2020.[6] This is consistent with earlier Commerce Department calculations estimating that in 2008, US.-Mexico border delays cost $6 billion in lost output and 26,000 lost jobs, and they will cost twice as much in 2017.[7]

Companies also complain about delays: for example, while 10+2 could be seen as an opportunity to optimize inefficient business processes and sharpen companies' competitive advantage, importers have voiced concerns that the rule adds a significant additional burden to trade compliance.[8]

Indeed, trade compliance—establishing a product's Harmonized System code; determining the product's customs duty rate, other import taxes, and rules of origin; verifying any restrictions or license requirements for the product; confirming documentation needed for import or exports; analyzing procedures for return of repaired or refurbished goods; and so on—is very challenging. This compliance is especially difficult for smaller American companies, especially as these rules vary extensively across foreign markets. In a 2010 U.S. International Trade Commission survey of 2,349 U.S. SMEs and 500 large firms, customs procedures topped the list of burdensome nontariff barriers to SMEs. Over

---

4. Vivian C. Jones and Marc R. Rosenblum, "U.S. Customs and Border Protection: Trade Facilitation, Enforcement, and Security," Congressional Research Service, March 22, 2013, http://fas.org/sgp/crs/homesec/R43014.pdf.

5. Ibid.

6. Amanda J. Crawford, "Border Delays Cost U.S. $7.8 Billion as Fence Is Focus," Bloomberg, May 14, 2013, http://www.bloomberg.com/news/2013-05-15/border-delays-cost-u-s-7-8-billion-as-fence-is-focus.html.

7. U.S. Department of Commerce, *Draft Report: Improving Economic Outcomes by Reducing Border Delays, Facilitating the Vital Flow of Commercial Traffic Across the US-Mexican Border* (Washington, DC: Department of Commerce, March 2008), 3, http://grijalva.house.gov/uploads/Draft%20Commerce%20Department%20Report%20on%20Reducing%20Border%20Delays%20Findings%20and%20Options%20March%202008.pdf.

8. See, for example, Matt Gersper, "CBP's 10+2 Readiness . . . Beware! It's strategic, not tactical!" *IIEI GlobalWatch* 10, issue 2 (September/October 2008), http://www.dunlap-stone.edu/globalwatch/2008_September-October.pdf.

62 percent of U.S. small and midsize manufacturers and 65 percent of large manufacturers stated that customs procedures posed "some burden," while almost 50 percent of SMEs and 30 percent of large companies said customs procedures pose "a major burden" (Figures 1 and 2).[9]

These patterns are echoed in a U.S. ITC survey of 3,466 companies in digitally intensive industries, of which some 80 percent were SMEs.[10] Manufacturing SMEs were the most likely among all SME firms to see customs requirements as impeding trade to some degree, with 48 percent of SMEs seeing customs requirements as an obstacle of varying degrees (Figure 3). Large retailers tended to view customs requirements as an obstacle, with 39 percent viewing them as a "substantial or very substantial" obstacle (Figure 4).

The reality is that the government does not currently have the capacity to scan all cargo entering the United States. New technologies developed by companies such as Decision Sciences could enable higher scanning rates at a minimal time of 30 to 40 seconds per container, compared to the minutes it takes for X-ray scanners.[11] However, the cost of the technology would be borne by foreign governments that operate scanning systems at their ports, something the European Union (EU) and China have refused to do.[12] So far, CBP has managed the trade-off between trade facilitation and scanning through ATS's risk targeting. However, questions about security will likely amplify given that a number of analysts believe that man-made attacks and cyber security threats are increasing in supply chains.[13]

LOW C-TPAT UPTAKE

The second challenge facing the customs regime is companies' low adoption of C-TPAT. On paper, C-TPAT has a number of benefits: acceding companies can face fewer inspections, secure expedited cargo releases, reduce their transit time, obtain priority processing for inspections that are required, be recognized as a safe and secure business, and improve their supply chain security. Yet only some 2.4 percent of U.S. importers and fewer than 10 percent of all customs brokers have joined the program.[14]

One reason for the low uptake is the program's rigorous requirements, which translate into real costs to companies. The minimum security criteria needed to apply for the program

9. U.S. International Trade Commission (ITC), *Small and Medium-Sized Enterprises: Characteristics and Performance* (Washington, DC: ITC, November 2010), http://www.usitc.gov/publications/332/pub4189.pdf.

10. ITC, *Digital Trade in the U.S. and Global Economies, Part 2* (Washington, DC: USITC, August 2014), http://www.usitc.gov/publications/332/pub4485.pdf.

11. Mark Szakonyi, "100 Percent Container Scanning for US-Bound Cargo Remains Elusive," *Journal of Commerce*, February 27, 2014, http://www.joc.com/regulation-policy/import-and-export-regulations/us-import export-regulations/100-percent-container-scanning-us-bound-cargo-remains-elusive_20140227.html.

12. Ibid.

13. PricewaterhouseCoopers (PWC), *Transportation & Logistics 2030: Volume 4: Securing the supply chain* (n.p.: PWC, 2011), http://www.pwc.com/en_GX/gx/transportation-logistics/pdf/TL2030_vol.4_web.pdf.

14. These 10,000 include U.S. importers, U.S./Canada highway carriers; U.S./Mexico highway carriers; rail and sea carriers; licensed U.S. Customs brokers; U.S. marine port authority/terminal operators; U.S. freight consolidators; ocean transportation intermediaries and nonoperating common carriers; Mexican and Canadian manufacturers; and Mexican long-haul carriers. Importers are calculated here as 4,430 importers reportedly in the program on September 1, 2014, as a share of all U.S. importers, reported at about 185,700 in the latest census.

Figure 1. Percent of U.S. SME Manufacturers Experiencing Nontariff Measures as Burdensome, 2010

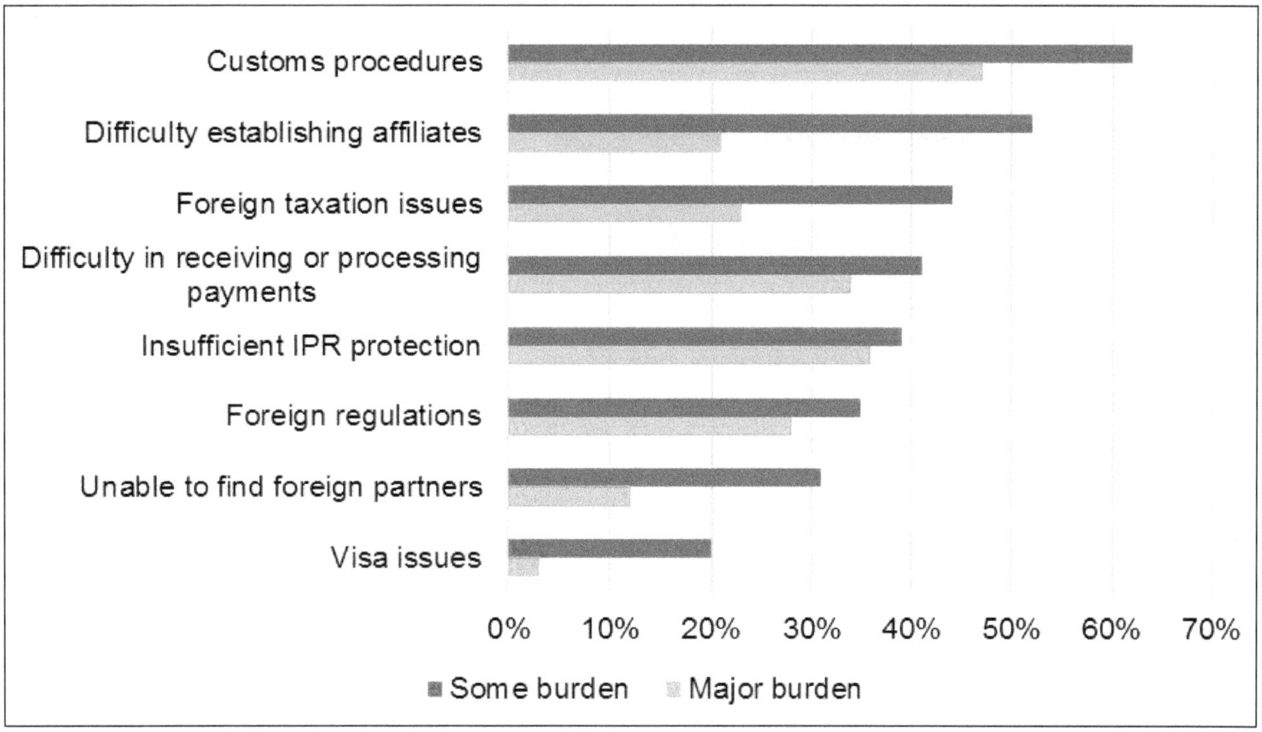

Data source: U.S. International Trade Commission (ITC), *Small and Medium-Sized Enterprises: Characteristics and Performance* (Washington, DC: ITC, November 2010).

Figure 2. Percent of Large U.S. Manufacturers Experiencing Nontariff Measures as Burdensome, 2010

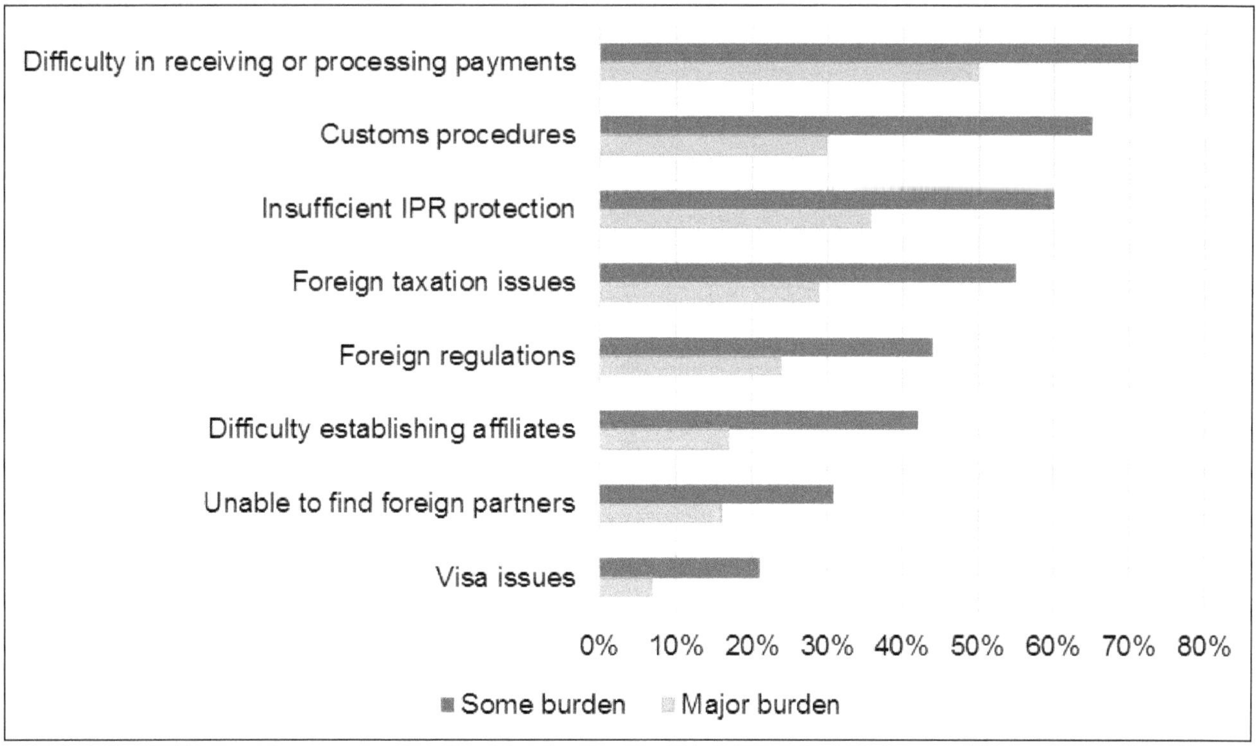

Data source: ITC, *Small and Medium-Sized Enterprises: Characteristics and Performance.*

Figure 3. SMEs' Perceptions That Customs Requirements Present an Obstacle to Digital Trade, by Sector and Firm Size (sorted by "substantial hurdle")

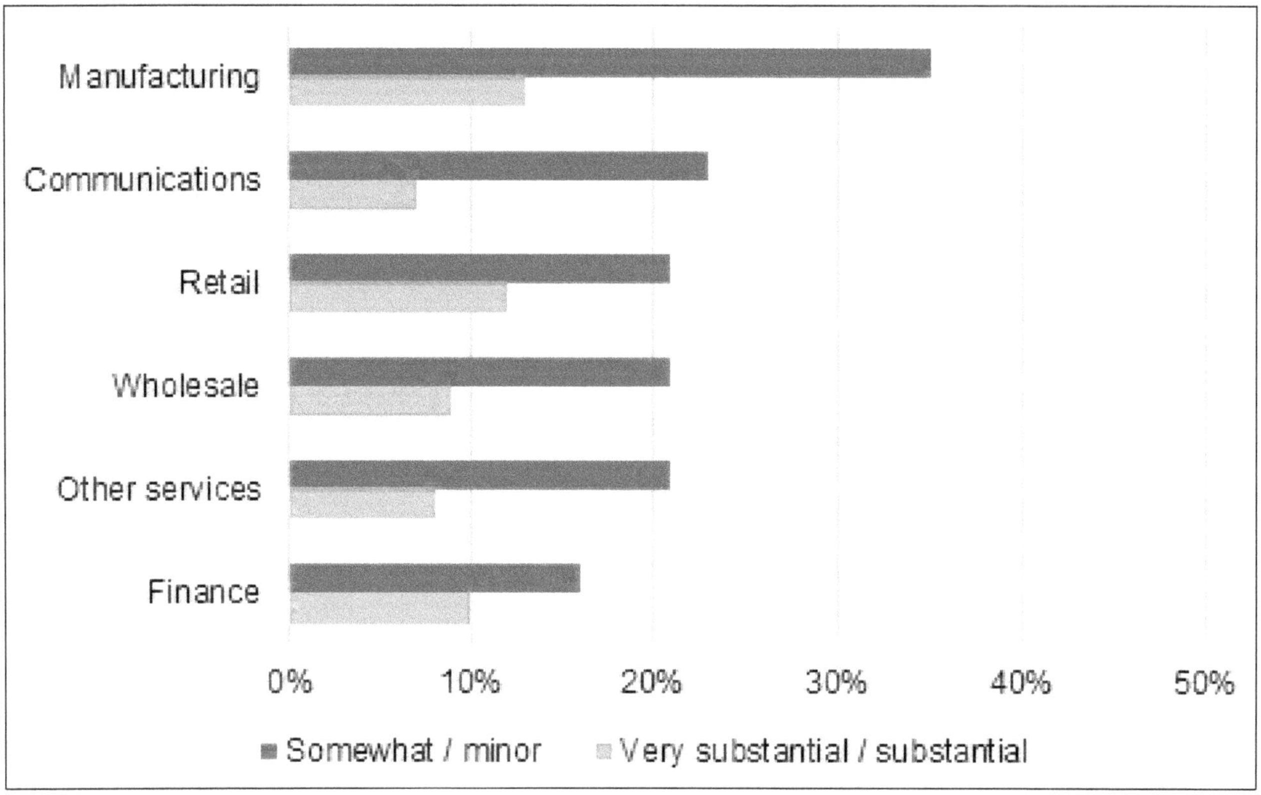

Data source: ITC, *Digital Trade in the U.S. and Global Economies, Part 2* (Washington, DC: ITC, August 2014).

Figure 4. Large Companies' Perceptions That Customs Requirements Present an Obstacle to Digital Trade, by Sector and Firm Size (sorted by "substantial hurdle")

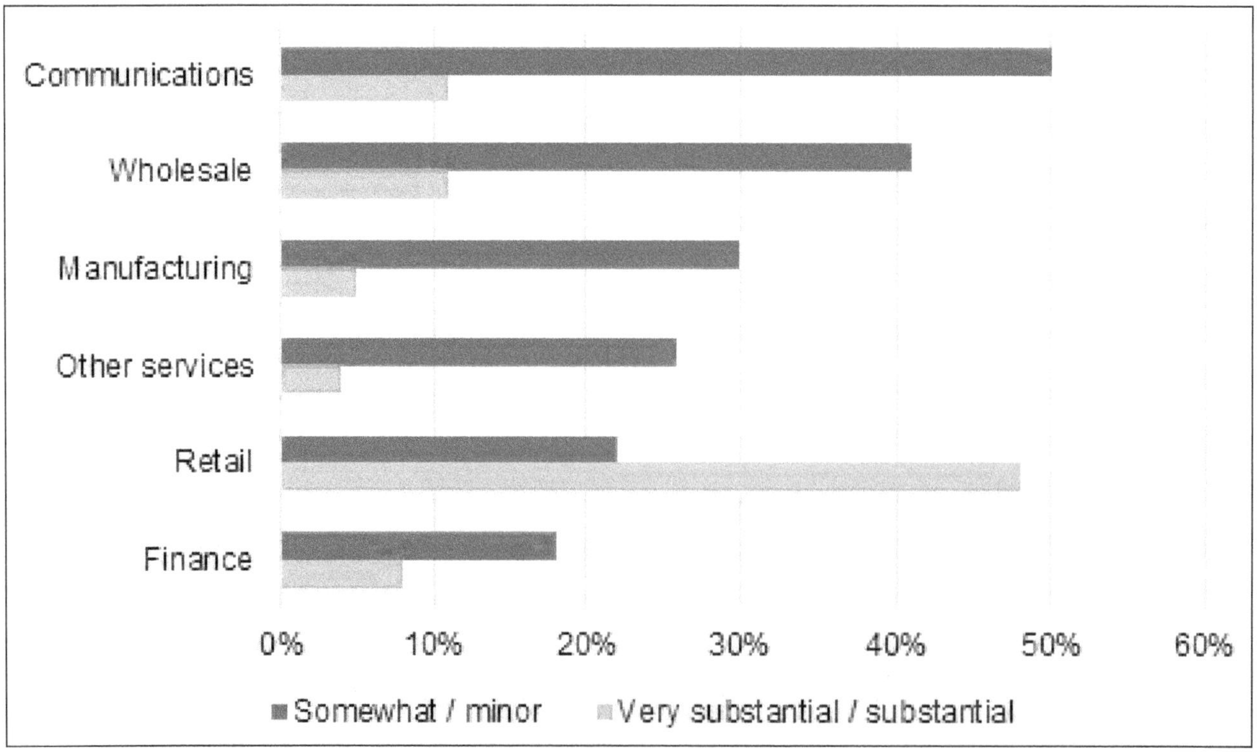

Data source: ITC, *Digital Trade in the U.S. and Global Economies, Part 2*.

Table 2. C-TPAT Minimum Security Criteria for Importers and Exporters

Importers	*Exporters*
• Be an active U.S. importer or nonresident Canadian importer into the United States. • Have a business office staffed in the United States or Canada. • Have an active U.S. importer of record ID in either of the following formats: U.S. Social Security Number, U.S. Internal Revenue Service assigned ID(s), or CBP assigned Importer ID. • Possess a valid continuous import bond registered with CBP. • Have a designated company officer that will be the primary cargo security officer responsible for C-TPAT. • Commit to maintaining the C-TPAT supply chain security criteria as outlined in the C-TPAT importer agreement. • Create and provide CBP with a C-TPAT supply chain security profile, which identifies how the importer will meet, maintain, and enhance internal policy to meet the C-TPAT importer security criteria. • Have at least one staffed business office in either of the two countries; have a very low volume of importers (less than 24 importations) for consideration on a case by case basis.	• Be an active U.S. exporter out of the United States. • Have a business office staffed in the United States. • Be an active U.S. exporter with a documentable Employer Identification Number (EIN) or Dun & Bradstreet (DUNS) number. • Have a documented export security program and a designated officer or manager who will act as the C-TPAT program main point of contact. • Commit to maintaining the C-TPAT supply chain security criteria as outlined in the C- TPAT exporter agreement. • Create and provide CBP with a C-TPAT supply chain security profile which identifies how the exporter will meet, maintain, and enhance internal policy to meet the C-TPAT exporter security criteria. • In order to be eligible, the exporter must have an acceptable level of compliance for export reporting for the latest 12-month period and be in good standing with U.S. regulatory bodies, such as the Department of Commerce, Department of State, Department of Treasury, Nuclear Regulatory Commission, Drug Enforcement Administration, and Department of Defense.

Source: Jones and Rosenblum, "U.S. Customs and Border Protection."

are not necessarily too difficult to meet (Table 2), but the several requirements for entering and remaining in the program are challenging (Table 3, Appendixes A and B). Both importers and exporters need to meet numerous criteria related to the sealing and securing of containers, physical security of the company's premises, threat awareness training for the company's employees, personnel security, procedural security, tracking and monitoring of the cargo that is transported, and so on. Companies have expressed concerns with the program's one-size-fits-all requirements.[15]

Another reason for the scant uptake of C-TPAT may be the limited benefits applicants would score vis-à-vis non-C-TPAT companies: while the 58 CSI ports prescreen over 80 percent of all maritime containerized cargo imported into the United States, only 4 percent of all

15. Jones and Rosenblum, "U.S. Customs and Border Protection."

Table 3. Select C-TPAT Requirements for Importers and Exporters

Importers	*Exporters*
• Where an importer outsources or contracts elements of their supply chain, such as a foreign facility, conveyance, domestic warehouse, or other elements, the importer must work with these business partners to ensure that pertinent security measures are in place and adhered to throughout their supply chain. • Importers must have written and verifiable processes for the selection of business partners including manufacturers, product suppliers, and vendors. • For those business partners not eligible for C-TPAT certification, importers must require their business partners to demonstrate that they are meeting C-TPAT security criteria via written/electronic confirmation (e.g., a written statement from the business partner demonstrating their compliance with C-TPAT security criteria or an equivalent WCO accredited security program administered by a foreign customs authority). Non-C-TPAT eligible business partners must be subject to verification of compliance with C-TPAT security criteria by the importer. • Cargo handling and storage facilities in domestic and foreign locations must have physical barriers and deterrents that guard against unauthorized access. Importers should incorporate C-TPAT physical security criteria throughout their supply chains as applicable. • Container integrity must be maintained to protect against the introduction of unauthorized material and/or persons. At point of stuffing, procedures must be in place to properly seal and maintain the integrity of the shipping containers. • Procedures must be in place to verify the physical integrity of the container structure prior to stuffing, to include the reliability of the locking mechanisms of the doors. A seven-point inspection process is recommended for all containers. • Proper vendor ID and/or photo identification must be presented for documentation purposes upon arrival by all vendors. Arriving packages and mail should be periodically screened before being disseminated.	• Must have an acceptable level of compliance for export reporting for the latest 12-month period and be in good standing with U.S. regulatory bodies. • Must have written and verifiable processes for the screening and selection of business partners including service providers, manufacturers, product suppliers, and vendors. • Periodic reviews of business partners' processes and facilities should be conducted based on risk to maintain the security standards required by the exporter. • Procedures must be in place to verify the physical integrity of the container structure prior to stuffing, to include the reliability of the locking mechanisms of the doors. A seven-point inspection process is recommended for all containers. • The sealing of export containers, to include continuous seal integrity, is a crucial element of a secure supply chain and remains a critical part of an exporter's commitment to C-TPAT. • Access controls to prevent unauthorized entry to cargo facilities must include the positive identification of all employees, visitors, service providers, and vendors at all points of entry. Perimeter fencing should enclose the areas around cargo handling and storage facilities. • Predetermined routes should be identified by the transportation provider for the exporter, and these procedures should consist of random route checks by the transportation provider along with documenting and verifying the length of time between the loading point/trailer pickup, the export point, and/or the delivery destinations, during peak and nonpeak times. • Processes must be in place to screen prospective employees and to periodically check current employees. • Procedures must be in place to prevent, detect, or deter undocumented material and unauthorized personnel from gaining access to conveyance, including concealment in containers.

Source: Jones and Rosenblum, "U.S. Customs and Border Protection."

maritime containers are selected for secondary inspection and experience delays.[16] This means that C-TPAT membership may offer limited practical advantages for companies.[17]

CHALLENGES OF MUTUAL RECOGNITION

The third challenge facing the customs regime is international—one of harmonization and mutual recognition of C-TPAT with other trusted trader and AEO programs. Under mutual recognition, C-TPAT and the foreign program have standardized security requirements, and one program may recognize the validation findings of the other program. Companies participating in these programs are given a reduced risk score, and their foreign suppliers will be less likely to be visited by C-TPAT.

However, mutual recognition is neither universal nor easy to establish, as the U.S. counterpart has to have sophisticated procedures and rules commensurate to those of CBP. As of September 1, 2014, C-TPAT had eight mutual recognition arrangements, with New Zealand, Canada, Jordan, Japan, Korea, European Union, Taiwan, and Israel. Together, these represent about one-half of U.S. imports. CBP also has four mutual recognition projects, two with its first and third largest sources of imports, China and Mexico, as well as with Singapore and Switzerland. There are also 12 technical assistance projects with India, Turkey, Jamaica, Dominican Republic, Honduras, Panama, Colombia, Chile, Peru, Uruguay, Brazil, and Costa Rica.

The mushrooming B2C and C2C trade of millions of small parcels crisscrossing the globe amplifies each of these three challenges. Before assessing these challenges, it is useful to understand how tomorrow's traders are different from the traditional exporters and importers. The following section takes a closer look.

16. Granted, implementation of the Container Security Initiative has faced challenges, including due to political issues with the foreign partner countries. The Government Accountability Office (GAO) found that CSI did not have a presence at about half of the ports Customs and Border Protection considered high risk and about one-fifth of the existing CSI ports were at lower risk locations. Since CSI depends on cooperation from sovereign host countries, there are challenges to implementing CSI in new foreign locations, and CBP's negotiations with other countries have not always succeeded. For example, CBP officials said it is difficult to close CSI ports and open new ports because removing CSI from a country might negatively affect U.S. relations with the host government. See GAO, "DHS Could Improve Cargo Security by Periodically Assessing Risks from Foreign Ports," September 2013, http://www.gao.gov/assets/660/657893.pdf.

17. Jones and Rosenblum, "U.S. Customs and Border Protection."

3 | The New Face of Trade: Exporters and Importers, Today and Tomorrow

So far, only a select few U.S. companies engage in trade, and it is the very largest companies that make up the bulk of U.S. trade flows. According to the latest census data, in 2012, 304,867 companies were exporters. This figure comprises a mere 1 percent of all U.S. businesses and 5 percent of employment-providing businesses (Figure 5). There were even fewer importers (185,729) in 2012 (Figure 6). Some 80,000 companies were two-way traders—exporters that also import.

U.S. trade, just as trade in most economies, is highly skewed towards large companies. Companies with 500 employees or more represent a small share of the number of companies, yet a lion's share of exports. In 2012, large exporters made up 2 percent of the number of U.S. exporters but 67 percent of American export volumes, as well as 3 percent of U.S. importers and 69 percent of U.S. imports.

Online buyers and sellers are different from offline sellers in many ways. They are technologically savvy and intrepid in using online tools to market, sell, and purchase products. But they are also very different from traditional players in their engagement in international trade:

- Online sellers are highly likely to export. On average, 97 percent of American micro and small businesses that sell on eBay also export, in stark contrast to the 1 percent of U.S. small businesses that export in the traditional "offline" way (Figure 7). This drastic difference between off- and online sellers occurs in other advanced nations as well as in developing countries. Online platforms dramatically expand buyers' visibility of sellers even far away: sellers' products are clearly visible and easy to explore across oceans. Online platforms' star ratings systems, customer reviews, and payment tools such as Paypal give the buyer a sense of trust, the lubricant of trade that in the offline economy takes several transactions between buyer and seller to build.
- In online trade, tools and visibility are similar for all companies, irrespective of their size. As such, small and large online sellers are almost equally likely to export and export as much. Even the smallest 10 percent of commercial eBay sellers

Figure 5. U.S. Exporters' Number and Share of Total Exporters and Imports, by Number of Employees

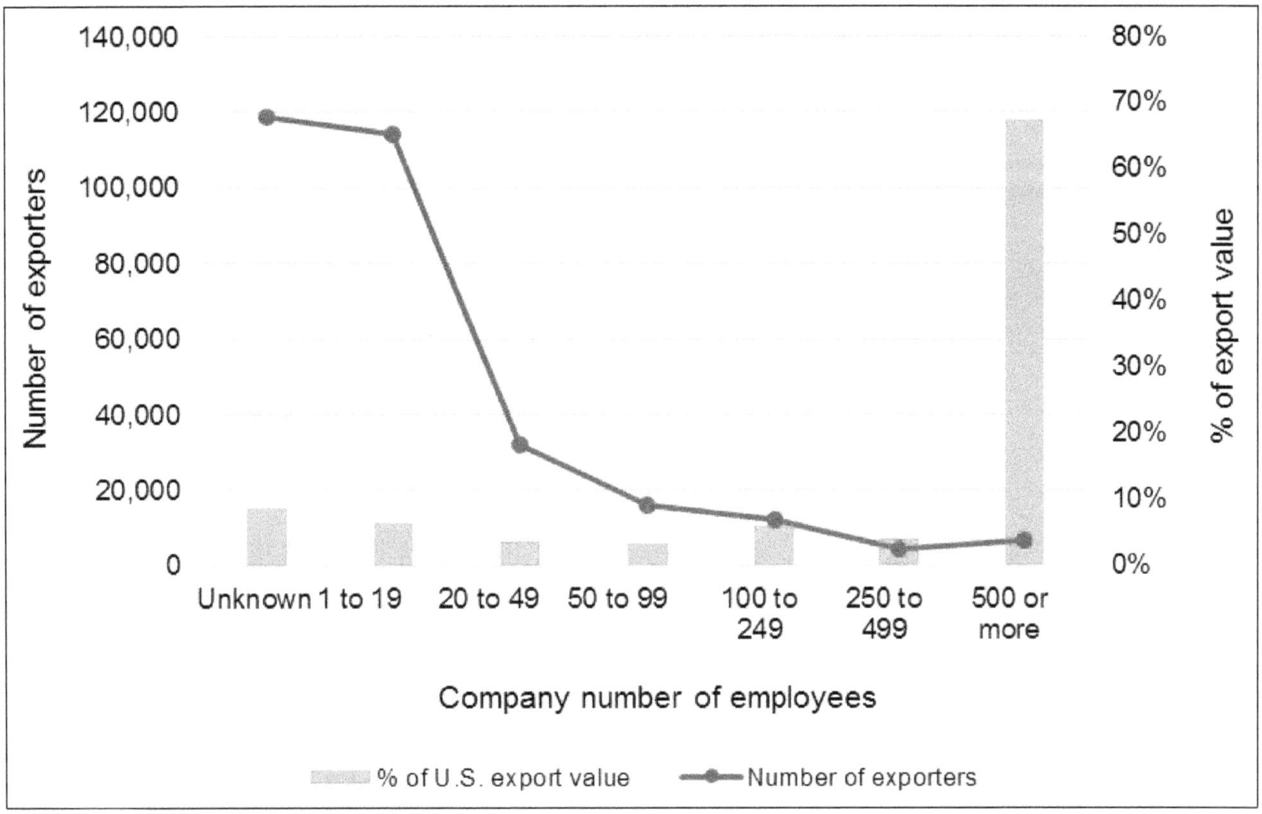

Data source: U.S. Census Bureau, "A Profile of U.S. Importing and Exporting Companies, 2011–2012," April 3, 2014, http://www.census.gov/foreign-trade/Press-Release/edb/2012/#full.

Figure 6. U.S. Importers' Number and Share of Total Exporters and Imports, by Number of Employees

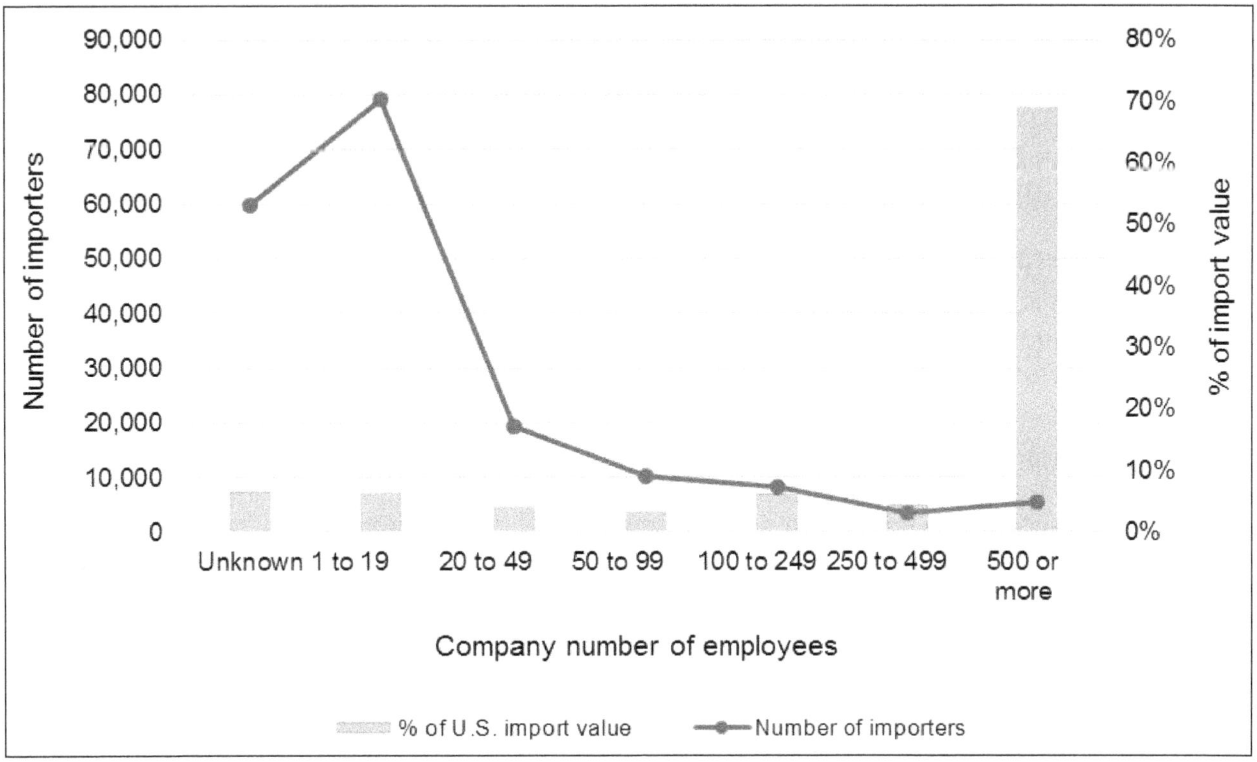

Data source: U.S. Census Bureau, "A Profile of U.S. Importing and Exporting Companies, 2011–2012."

Figure 7. Share of Sellers Exporting on eBay vs. Offline

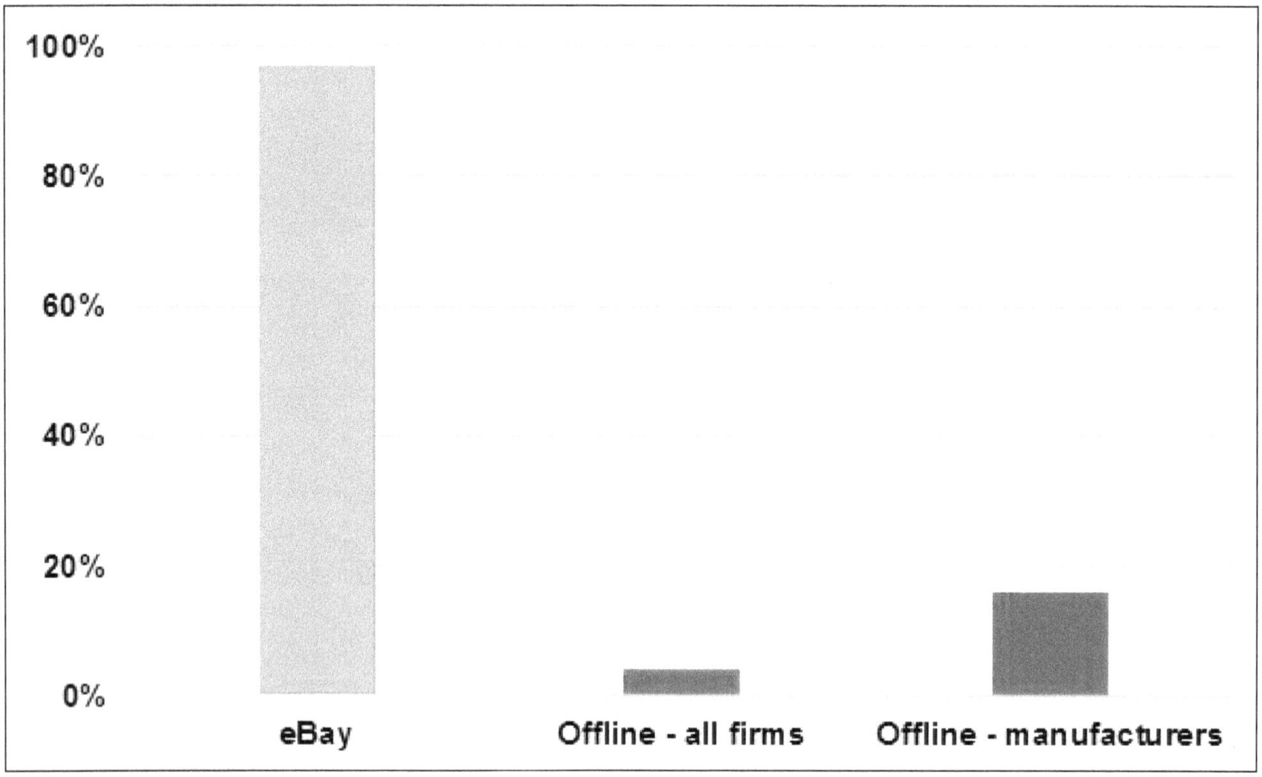

Data source: eBay, *Enabling Traders to Enter and Grow on the Global Stage* (Washington, DC: eBay, October 2012), http://www.ebaymainstreet.com/sites/default/files/EBAY_US-Marketplace_FINAL.pdf.

overwhelmingly engage in exports, with 94 percent exporting (Figure 8). For these small sellers, exports make up 14 percent of all sales—not very different from the levels for the largest seller, for which exports make up 18 percent of all sales. In addition, while U.S. exports, just like almost every country's exports, have traditionally been driven by the largest companies, on online platforms small exporters play a much more elevated role in driving trade: they tend to make up a much larger share of all exports made online than of exports offline.

- Online exporters and importers are typically smaller than "offline" exporters and importers: even the largest online exporters on eBay pale before those of the largest corporate exporters.[1] Online importers and exports also tend to be quite new to import and export and to have irregular, sporadic shipments. As a result, they have much more limited operating track-records and paper trails of trade transactions and compliance than do large, seasoned exporters and importers.
- In cross-border online trade, the importer of record is typically an individual consumer, and the exporter is frequently a small business. These actors have much more

1. eBay, *Enabling Traders to Enter and Grow on the Global Stage* (Washington, DC: eBay, October 2012), http://www.ebaymainstreet.com/sites/default/files/EBAY_US-Marketplace_FINAL.pdf.

Figure 8. Share of Sellers Exporting and Share of Value Exported, by Deciles

Data source: eBay, *Enabling Traders to Enter and Grow on the Global Stage.*

limited capabilities and knowledge about customs regulations than large corporations do. The fixed costs involved with shipping, trade compliance, and other factors can thus more easily usurp the profits of small businesses than is the case for large companies that tend to ship in bulk: small business trade is highly sensitive to the costs of trading across borders.

- Trade compliance costs matter a great deal more to online than offline exporters because of the diversification of their export markets. As opposed to the more than 50 percent of U.S. offline exporters that export to one or two countries, 81 percent of online exporters export to five or more countries (Figure 9). The diversification is very substantial: the smallest 10 percent of U.S. regular online exporters on eBay serve 28 markets on average, and the largest 10 percent sell to 66 different markets (Figure 10). This means these companies face multiple distinct trade compliance regimes, a maze for a small business to manage.

How important are these online sellers in U.S. exports? Perhaps the best recent estimate is by U.S. ITC, which calculates that firms in digitally intensive industries exported a total of $223 billion in products and services ordered online in 2012. The top two sectors for exports of products and services ordered online were manufacturing ($87 billion or 39 percent) and digital communications ($59 billion or 26 percent).[2] These figures are poised to grow quite fast in light of the expansion of online shopping around the world.

2. U.S. International Trade Commission (ITC), *Digital Trade in the U.S. and Global Economies, Part 2* (Washington, DC: ITC, August 2014), http://www.usitc.gov/publications/332/pub4485.pdf.

Figure 9. Number of Export Destinations: Small vs. Large eBay Exporters (sellers with > $10,000 in exports)

Data source: eBay, *Enabling Traders to Enter and Grow on the Global Stage.*

Figure 10. Number of Export Destinations, eBay Sellers with > $10,000 Exports, by Deciles of Sales Value

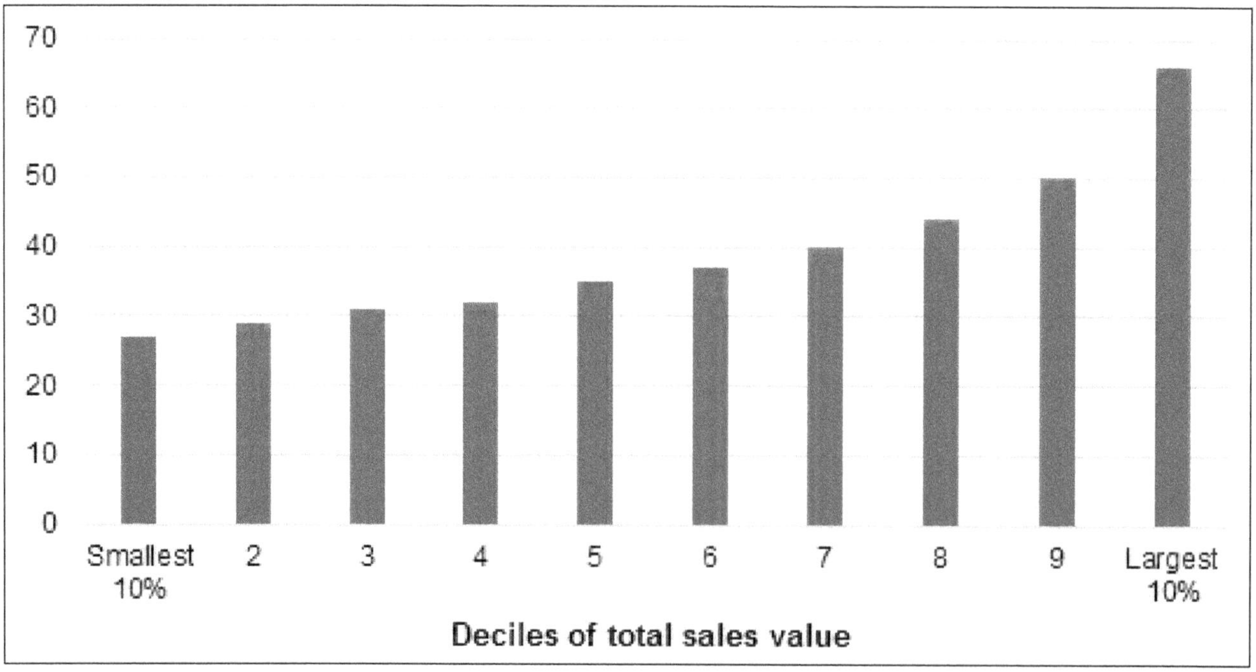

Data source: eBay, *Enabling Traders to Enter and Grow on the Global Stage.*

Figure 11. Top Regions for Exports of Products and Services Ordered Online, by Percentage of Firms, 2012

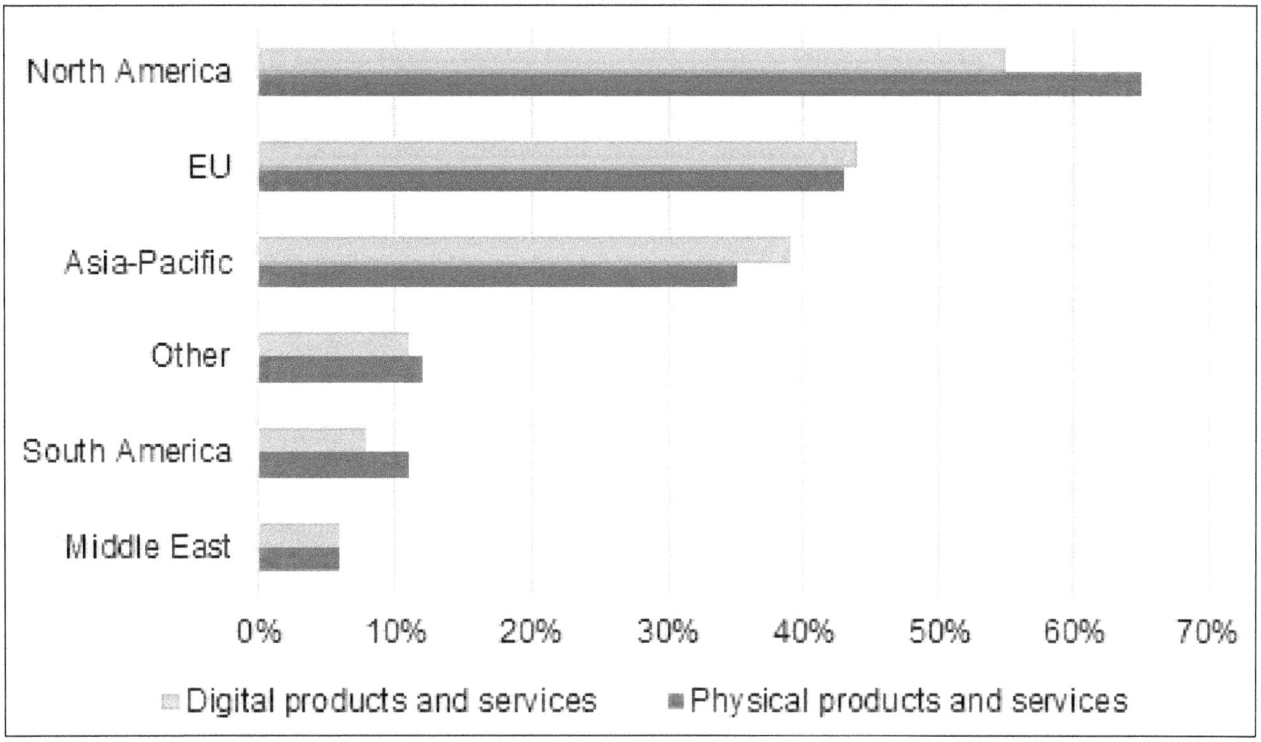

Data source: U.S. International Trade Commission (ITC), *Digital Trade in the U.S. and Global Economies, Part 2* (Washington, DC: ITC, August 2014), http://www.usitc.gov/publications/332/pub4485.pdf.

The top destinations for both digitally and physically delivered U.S. exports that were ordered online were North America (primarily Canada), the European Union (primarily the UK), and the Asia-Pacific region (Australia and China) (Figure 11).

The value of imports ordered online by U.S. companies in digitally intensive industries was $106 billion, with 94 percent delivered physically rather than digitally to U.S. buyers.[3] Firms in manufacturing ($51 billion), digital communications ($23 billion), and retail trade ($18 billion) had the largest shares of digitally and physically delivered imports that had been ordered online in 2012 (Figure 12).

Enabling U.S. companies to export to a vaster market and U.S. consumers to access a wider variety of products at the lowest cost, digital trade enhances U.S. productivity, economic growth, and job creation. Even under U.S. ITC's narrower sectoral definition, digital trade—domestic commerce and international trade conducted via the Internet—increased U.S. GDP by 3.4 to 4.8 percent in 2011, U.S. real wages by 4.5 to 5 percent, and created up to 2.4 million new full-time jobs.[4]

3. Ibid.
4. Ibid.

Figure 12. Imports of Products and Services Online by Sector and Delivery Mode, 2012 (in billions of US$)

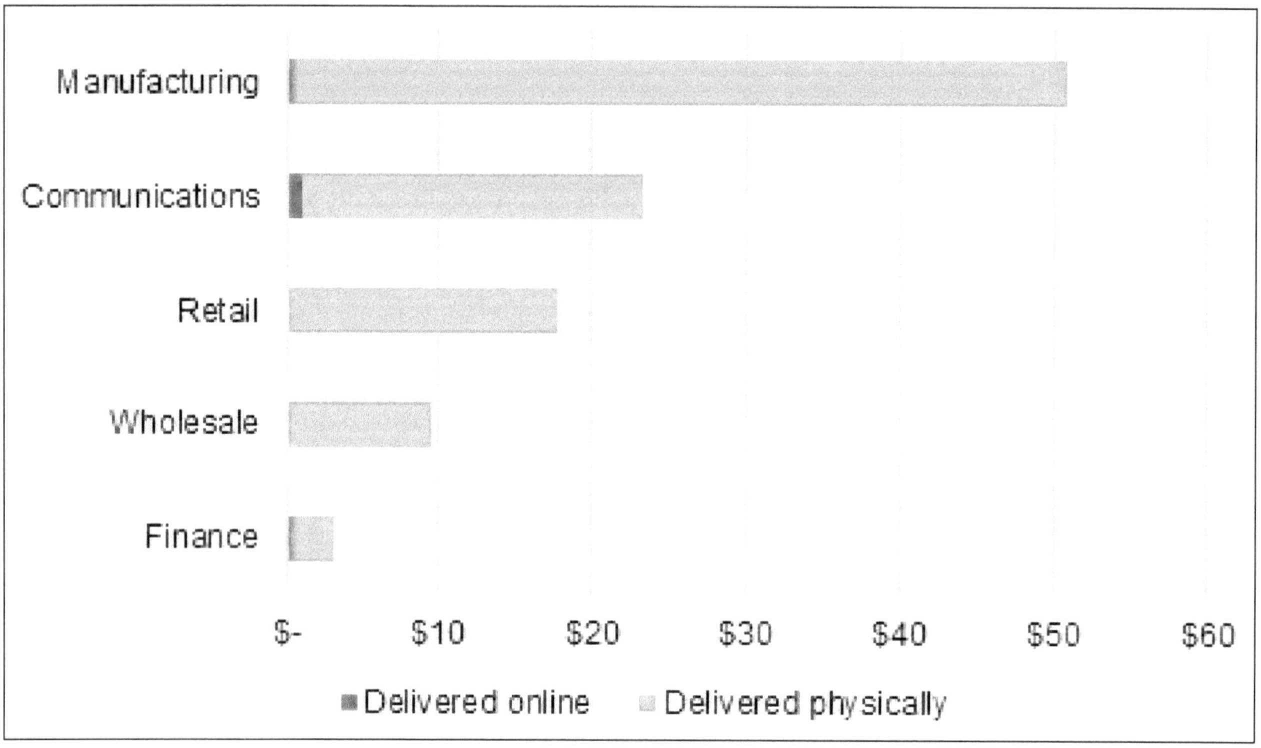

Data source: ITC, *Digital Trade in the U.S. and Global Economies, Part 2.*

Rapid Growth of E-commerce Opportunities

Granted, not all companies engage in online trade; globally, most companies have yet to get online or establish websites or e-commerce platforms. However, e-commerce is soaring around the world. Already, some 2.6 billion people, or 38 percent of the world's population, use the Internet, and another 2 to 3 billion are forecast to access the web, typically through smart phones, by 2020, particularly in China, India, and Africa, as well as in Brazil and across South America. That more consumers get online should augment B2C and C2C transactions in particular, as well as open opportunities for U.S. small businesses and individuals to sell and buy goods and services around the world. Globally, B2C transactions are expected to soar to $2.4 trillion in 2017 from $1.5 trillion in 2014 (Figure 13 and Table 4), with China leading the way.

Also, cross-border e-commerce will surge. U.S. cross-border e-commerce transactions are expected to double to $80 billion between 2013 and 2017 (Figure 14). These numbers could well be higher as trade in digital products—such as 3D-printable parts and components—expands. The largest growth in cross-border transactions is in China, where they will make up an estimated $160 billion in 2018, up from $43 billion in 2013.

Figure 13. Global B2C E-commerce Marketplace in 2012–2017 (in billions of US$)

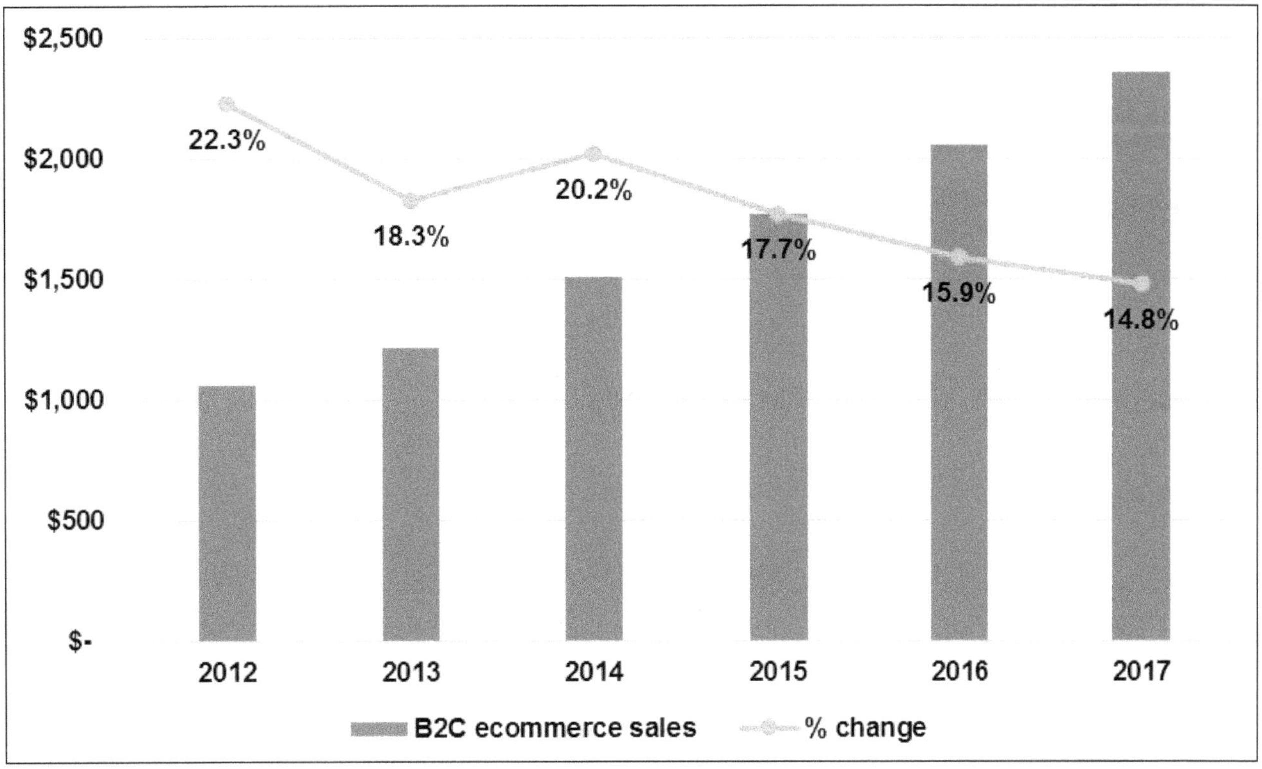

Data source: eMarketer, "Global B2C Ecommerce Sales to Hit $1.5 Trillion This Year Driven by Growth in Emerging Markets," February 3, 2014, http://www.emarketer.com/Article/Global-B2C-Ecommerce-Sales-Hit-15-Trillion-This-Year-Driven-by-Growth-Emerging-Markets/1010575.

Table 4. Global B2C E-commerce Marketplace in 2012–2017 (in billions of US$ and average annual growth), by Region

	2012	*2013*	*2014*	*2015*	*2016*	*2017*	*CAGR*
Asia Pacific	$301.2	$383.9	$525.2	$681.2	$855.7	$1,052.9	50%
North America	$379.8	$431.0	$482.6	$538.3	$597.9	$660.4	15%
Western Europe	$277.5	$312.0	$347.4	$382.7	$414.2	$445.0	12%
Central & Eastern Europe	$41.5	$49.5	$58.0	$64.4	$68.9	$73.1	15%
Latin America	$37.6	$48.1	$57.7	$64.9	$70.6	$74.6	20%
Middle East & Africa	$20.6	$27.0	$33.8	$39.6	$45.5	$51.4	30%
Worldwide	$1,058	$1,215	$1,505	$1,771	$2,053	$2,357	25%

Data source: eMarketer, "Global B2C Ecommerce Sales to Hit $1.5 Trillion This Year Driven by Growth in Emerging Markets."

Given the popularity of U.S. e-commerce sites, the rise in global online trade is poised to boost U.S. exports. A 2013 survey of individual cross-border online shoppers in the United States, Australia, Brazil, China, Germany, and UK showed that U.S. e-commerce sites were the most popular destination, cited by 45 percent of the online shoppers, followed by the

Figure 14. Cross-Border E-commerce Marketplace in 2018 (in billions of US$), by Country

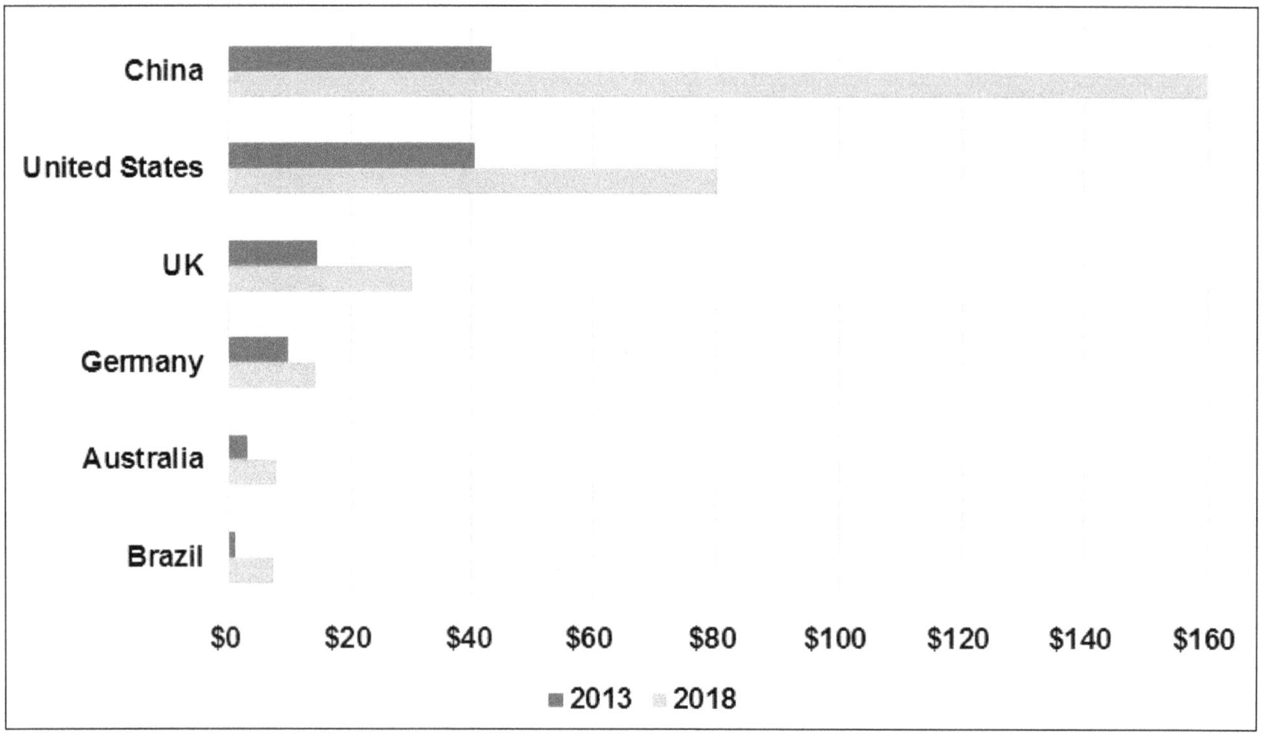

Data source: Paypal, "Modern Spice Routes: The Cultural Impact and Economic Opportunity of Cross-Border Shopping," 2013, https://www.paypal-media.com/assets/pdf/fact_sheet/PayPal_ModernSpiceRoutes_Report_Final.pdf.

United Kingdom at 37 percent, China at 26 percent, Hong Kong at 25 percent, Canada at 18 percent, Australia at 16 percent, and Germany at 14 percent.[5] The United States was the most popular market for shoppers in each of the other five countries; the most popular country for U.S. cross-border online shoppers was the United Kingdom, followed by China and Canada. The most cited reason for buying from a foreign e-commerce site was to save money, cited by 80 percent of respondents, followed by finding goods not available locally, mentioned by 79 percent.

Implications of the Expansion of E-commerce on Customs Security

These above stylized facts about online trade and traders have five implications.

First, international trade is more diffuse than ever, spread across the millions of companies and consumers that participate in cross-border online trade, creating billions of

5. Don Davis, "Millions of consumers cross virtual borders to shop online," *Internet Retailer*, July 23, 2013, http://www.internetretailer.com/2013/07/23/millions-consumers-cross-virtual-borders-shop-online.

micro-transactions and trade in small parcels. This does not necessarily mean that risk is also more diffuse—after all, a small parcel arguably poses a much lower security risk than large containers do when released to the U.S. soil. What it can mean, however, is that risks—of contraband, arms smuggling, narcotics, and other illicit activity—are more opaque, given that governments have more limited visibility into small online sellers and buyers. Customs regimes must now address these unique challenges posed by the changing landscape of participants in trade.

Second, in the world of online trade, governments cannot possibly physically inspect every parcel that crosses borders. This puts a premium on robust data, predictive analytics, and risk targeting as the key pillars of customs security. After all, not all shipments are equal: certain types of shipments from certain countries should be subjected to more rigid scrutiny. Yet, governments have far less visibility into data on the emerging players in trade that often make sporadic transactions than they do on the traditional drivers of trade: large multinational companies that make regular import-export shipments of specific commodities.

Third, existing government security programs such as C-TPAT are tailored to large companies shipping large volumes and staffed to meet complex trade compliance requirements, not small exporters and importers with limited compliance capabilities. One-size-fits-all customs regimes will not work in tomorrow's trade. New customs regimes have to be designed to reflect the rise of small business in trade, as well as the fact that many individual consumers are now importers of record.

Fourth, small businesses have scant incentives to seek to meet C-TPAT for expedited entry, in light of the program's high costs and limited benefits and the convenience of the status quo. A small subset of players may qualify for the duty-free, fast-tracked treatment for shipments below a certain value threshold and would not be subject to customs procedures. However, as in most countries, U.S. de minimis is very low at $200. Another subset may benefit from an "informal entry" regime, where incoming shipments below $2,500 can benefit from expedited customs clearance not needing a surety bond and having reduced paperwork requirements. Still, full manifest detail and prearrival information are required for all shipments, regardless of declared value.

Fifth, the growth in e-commerce will also accentuate the importance of international coordination in customs security and trade facilitation. One reason is simply that all countries are seeing the same increases in trade led by small businesses and individuals—and struggling with the balance of customs security and trade facilitation. Another reason is that any new security regime aimed at small online importers and exporters would need to be acceptable to U.S. trading partners in order to truly facilitate trade. For example, the European Union and the United States would probably need to strike another mutual recognition agreement, above and beyond what has been accomplished with AEO programs. More challenging, as e-commerce enables companies and consumers even in the most distant corners of the world to engage in trade, it is bound to expand U.S. trade with countries with which the prospects for mutual recognition are more limited.

In short, there is a mismatch between existing government security capabilities and the future of trade and between the existing trade compliance requirements and the capabilities and incentives of future traders. Customs regimes have been made for an era where only select U.S. companies engaged in trade; they are not well suited for tomorrow's trade. They neither facilitate it nor secure it well.

What needs to be recognized is that small businesses are not the only ones affected by the customs regimes designed for traditional trade: also affected are the countless large companies that increasingly use e-commerce to reach individual customers in foreign markets. Indeed, in many cases, large companies use e-commerce just like small companies do—as the key and even as the only means to access a foreign buyer. For example, while Wal-mart has struggled to open physical retail presence in India, it does use e-commerce to ship goods from other countries to Indian customers. Customs regimes for small parcels destined to small buyers is an issue for businesses of all sizes, not only small and medium-sized enterprises (SMEs).

Positively, online trade offers new opportunities for customs security, particularly in light of the massive amounts of electronic data on products, destinations, and volumes that online exporters leave behind, and the fact that online traders do their transactions online and are, as such, savvy users of the web and "e-trained." The key question is: How might data and technologies be leveraged better to mitigate risk in the future of trade? In particular, (1) how to best incentivize and help SMEs' meet customs requirements; (2) how to enhance governments' visibility into online trade; and (3) how to coordinate such efforts internationally? The following section lays out solutions.

4 | Customs Security Regime for the Future of Trade

Online trade is the trade of the twenty-first century. It has outstanding potential for expanding U.S. exports and entrepreneurship and boosting welfare around the world. However, online trade is still opaque and amorphous to governments. The key participants in online trade are small businesses and individuals who often lack a consistent track record in trading across borders, let alone a robust paper trail of consistent trade compliance.

On the one hand, the rise of small players in trade makes risk appear fragmented and amorphous. On the other, it accentuates the need for streamlined, low-cost trade compliance and customs procedures. The online revolution needs now to be matched by a twenty-first century customs security regime—one that addresses legitimate security concerns while accommodating the "shrinking" of participants in international trade. What follows is a vision for such a new security framework. This framework is envisioned to be piloted as an 18-month "eTrade Track," a comprehensive initiative run by CBP to secure and fuel small business and online trade that consists of the five main components outlined in the following paragraphs.

Enhancing Government's Data on Online Exporters and Importers

The first leg of eTrade Track is Big Data on online trade. Governments need greater transparency in online trade so as to facilitate the free flow of legitimate trade, while also gauging the type and degree of potential security risks posed by the new entrants in trade and detecting anomalies to target the most suspicious shipments and companies. Big Data, held primarily by major online platforms such as eBay and Alibaba, opens an opportunity for such risk targeting and predictive analytics in customs security. CBP should work with these intermediaries in a public-private dialogue aimed at discussing the e-commerce landscape, the data needs that customs services have, and the appropriate risk management models for e-commerce. This process could include a pilot program that leverages the Big Data in CBP's fieldwork.

Analysis of data on cross-border online transactions could reveal useful findings for allocating government resources in the most optimal fashion. For example, if the data show that most of the small online traders and their shipments are low risk, then the CBP would know to invest in buttressing the customs security regime in other areas.

The methodology for analyzing the data on cross-border transactions does not have to be based on existing models. Rather, it could draw on models aimed to assess risk in other areas where risk appears diffuse, such as in banking and finance. For example, the prepaid card industry's "red flags" include transactions such as high dollar deposits followed by numerous small withdrawals, large numbers of failed authorizations, repetitive transactions occurring at the same time for the same amount each day or each week, and multiple transactions slightly below reportable thresholds.[1] There are, however, three issues that will need to be worked out for the collaboration between customs and online platforms to work. The first is privacy: the data provided by online platforms to governments should not compromise the online sellers and buyers' private, company-specific data. Rather, it could include rather generic information such as the shipped product's Harmonized System code, value per shipment, mode of transport, seller's and buyer's locations, and number of times they import and export per year.[2]

The second issue is international coordination. To the extent the program is operationalized in the field, there would need to be prior discussions with those trading partners whose imports or exports could be affected. For example, a CBP-led pilot could focus on transatlantic trade, with data and procedures being shared with the EU officials.

The third issue is the fact that many small business online sellers are multichannel—they may use eBay, Amazon, and other platforms in addition to their own websites. While challenging, data and risk-based screening should be comprehensive, taking into account transactions across the different platforms. The exercise should also cover small businesses that use their own websites rather than, or in addition to, an intermediary platform.

Enhancing SMEs' Customs Filing and Trade Compliance

The second leg of the eTrade Track is a voluntary program for small online sellers and buyers to file basic trade compliance data so as to start building a paper trail and confidence with governments. Given that online businesses have limited incentives and capabilities to meet complex customs security requirements, there is a need for a customs compliance program that (1) gives governments minimum necessary data for customs security purposes; (2) enables online sellers and buyers to enter their compliance data in a quick and affordable fashion, without endless research; and (3) incentivizes the online

1. Network Branded Prepaid Card Association (NBPCA), *Recommended Practices for Anti-Money Laundering Compliance for U.S.-based Prepaid Cards Programs* (Montvale, NJ: NBPCA, 2008), http://www.nbpca.com/docs/nbpca-aml-recommended-practices-080220.pdf.

2. The author thanks Marianne Rowden of American Association for Exporters and Importers for these insights.

sellers and buyers to do so. This solution would also enhance transparency of the many small business that use their own e-commerce platform.

One solution is a customized trade compliance platform akin to TurboTax. Using the platform, which we will name "Turbo Trade" in this paper, exporters and importers would impute the relevant product's HS code, value shipped, and target (or source) market and then access customized information on the trade compliance rules pertinent to their produce. The platform would enable the company to provide compliance data required for the product and market in a brief fashion, in four to six data fields. Companies that build a consistent paper trail and comply consistently would over time become "Trusted eTraders" eligible for expedited entry. Complementing the platform could be a program to "train the trainers"—a low-cost program for trade compliance officers that could be used by several of the small online sellers. Such a compliance program does not need to be solely for online exporters and importers but could be used by SMEs more widely.

Listening to the Market: Feedback Site

Many challenges in trade go undetected; they are encountered by entrepreneurs and businesses each day, yet they remain uncatalogued. The eTrade Track can offer the new participants in trade an opportunity to send feedback akin to consumer complaint sites of problems and undue delays that companies face in customs or about positive experiences. CBP already has such a mechanism on its Info-site; this could now be leveraged for e-commerce.

Raising De Minimis and Informal Entry

Raising de minimis and informal entry levels would not undermine the quest for security, as full manifest detail and prearrival information is required for all shipments regardless of declared value. Raising de minimis from $200 to $800, as widely proposed across the trade community, and doubling informal entry to $5,000, would significantly reduce the time and paperwork for all parties in the trade supply chain—importers, express shippers, postal services—and free up resources for identifying serious threats from terrorism to counterfeit merchandise, illegal drugs, and food safety.

Raising de minimis would also impart economic gains. A Peterson Institute study estimates that the net payoff of an increase in the de minimis threshold to $800 for 3.8 million shipments in the $200 to $800 range handled by express shipment firms would be $17 million annually, taking into account the cost savings at each stage of the delivery chain and the revenue not collected by the customs authorities.[3] A higher de minimis could be piloted in eTrade Track for a subset of companies with which the government has a certain comfort level.

---

3. Gary Clyde Hufbauer and Yee Wong, "Logistics Reform for Low-Value Shipments," Policy Brief No. BP11-7, Peter G. Peterson Institute for International Economics, June 2011, http://www.iie.com/publications/pb/pb11-07.pdf.

Furthering International Cooperation and Mutual Recognition

The eTrade Track inherently needs to be bi- or multilateral to work. The United States might unilaterally put a world-class program in place, but it would benefit very little unless the main U.S. trading partners accept data and standards. There are three possible venues, all with voluminous trade and deep, preexisting cooperation on customs security measures.

- **APEC:** The Asia-Pacific Economic Cooperation forum has long had working groups for customs cooperation, trade facilitation, SMEs, and for the development of e-commerce. APEC's Electronic Commerce Steering Group (ECSG) promotes the development and use of electronic commerce by creating legal, regulatory, and policy environments in the APEC region. The United States could pilot the eTrack with a subset of APEC members with which the United States has had longer-standing customs cooperation and mutual recognition, such as Japan, Canada, Korea, and Taiwan.
- **NAFTA region:** The North American Free Trade Agreement region has extensive cooperation in customs procedures, standards harmonization, and other areas. It would be natural to expand this into customs cooperation to online trade. The starting point can be Canada, with which the United States has a mutual recognition agreement. The next step is Mexico, perhaps after the mutual recognition agreement with Mexico's AEO program is reached.
- **The transatlantic market:** The transatlantic market is the largest e-commerce marketplace as yet, and it will be solidified further through the Transatlantic Trade and Investment Partnership (TTIP) agreement, which will likely contain sophisticated disciplines on e-commerce. The United States and European Union have also had long-standing mutual recognition between C-TPAT and EU's AEO program that could be built upon.

Pacific Alliance as a Regional Pilot

The eTrade Track pilot program can also be tested in other world regions. One venue could be the Pacific Alliance, Latin America's newest integration bloc among Colombia, Chile, Mexico, and Peru, which finalized a free trade agreement in early 2014. Until recently, with separate bilateral FTAs with one another, the four members have freed tariffs on 92 percent of goods and services and established common rules of origin. The members have also abolished tourist visas, joined the members' stock exchanges through the Mercado Integrado de Latinoamérica (MILA), and consolidated embassies and commercial offices overseas. Integration of infrastructure, energy, and customs will follow.

The alliance is a significant market of 210 million consumers, 35 percent of Latin American GDP, and 55 percent of the region's exports. This market is growing: Costa Rica has signed an agreement to join the bloc, and Panama and Guatemala will follow. The region is ripe for expansion of e-commerce and for customs cooperation on online trade: the member economies have experienced explosive growth in mobile usage and e-commerce purchases in the past few years, have signed a cooperation agreement on e-commerce, and have established working groups promoting both trade and SMEs.

Notably, the United States has free trade agreements with all four economies, is an observer in the Pacific Alliance, and could work with the alliance toward a regional pilot program on e-commerce and customs security. What's more, given that Mexico, Chile, and Peru form part of APEC and TPP, the alliance's policy innovations could build momentum for new thinking on customs regimes in these broader transpacific fora.

5 Conclusion

The vast majority of small businesses that are using digital platforms to sell goods and services also engage in cross-border trade, in stark contrast to the world of traditional, offline trade where only a fraction of businesses export. Indeed, the costs of engaging in cross-border trade have never been so low nor the economic opportunities so large. Though large corporations will continue to be important to trade in the years ahead, individual consumers, small businesses, and garage entrepreneurs are the future face of trade.

The changes in the landscape of importers and exporters raise complex questions about customs security. Assessing the risks posed by small companies and microtransactions is hard because their trade transactions are often new and irregular, and thus they do not provide a steady stream of data like large companies do for governments to detect anomalies and target the most suspicious shipments and companies. However, given that customs services are highly unlikely to ever be able to scan all parcels exiting and entering countries for illicit arms, narcotics, and other contraband, it is critical for governments to find means to target businesses and parcels that can pose a security risk, while allowing legitimate trade to move freely.

Positively, online trade inherently leaves an electronic record of each transaction. Hence online platforms are placed to generate vast amounts of Big Data on the patterns of and participants in online trade that can be put to work in the interest of customs security. In addition, inherently e-trained, online traders can also be easily integrated into standardized e-compliance platforms.

This report has proposed the creation of an 18-month customs pilot program, eTrade Track, that leverages data and an online platform to secure and facilitate online trade. The envisioned eTrade Track has the following five legs:

- Big Data distilled by e-commerce platforms on online transactions and shared with customs for predictive analytics. In order to be successful, data collection and transfer must be done in a way that fully respects online sellers' and buyers' privacy.
- An online, custom Turbo Trade compliance program akin to TurboTax, where small businesses can immediately find a checklist of their unique compliance requirements and impute their required compliance information quickly and affordably. The incentive for companies is to build confidence and a paper trail with customs,

ultimately in exchange for an entry into a "Trusted eTrader" program for fast-tracked shipments.

- Bottom-up data gathering akin to consumer complaint sites of problems and undue delays that online sellers and buyers experience in customs.
- Increases in the level of de minimis and informal entries.
- Regionalized effort with key trading partners to pilot these ideas, such as with partners in APEC, NAFTA, the transatlantic market, and the Pacific Alliance—all arenas of voluminous trade with preexisting, deep cooperation on customs security measures.

The eTrade Track is a low-cost pilot that would start providing customs with visibility into the changing landscape of U.S. and world trade. It is a small investment in light of the gains that millions of American consumers and companies stand to reap from engaging in trade.

Appendix A. C-TPAT Importer Requirements

Importers must conduct a comprehensive assessment of their international supply chains based upon the following C-TPAT security criteria. Where an importer outsources or contracts elements of its supply chain, such as a foreign facility, conveyance, or domestic warehouse, the importer must work with these business partners to ensure that pertinent security measures are in place and adhered to throughout their supply chain. The supply chain for C-TPAT purposes is defined from point of origin (manufacturer/supplier/vendor) through to point of distribution and recognizes the diverse business models C-TPAT members employ. C-TPAT recognizes the complexity of international supply chains and endorses the application and implementation of security measures based upon risk analysis. Therefore, the program allows for flexibility and the customization of security plans based on the member's business model.

Appropriate security measures, as listed throughout this document, must be implemented and maintained throughout the importer's supply chains based on risk.

Business Partner Requirement

Importers must have written and verifiable processes for the selection of business partners, including manufacturers, product suppliers, and vendors.

Security Procedures

For those business partners eligible for C-TPAT certification (carriers, ports, terminals, brokers, consolidators, etc.), the importer must have documentation (e.g., C-TPAT certificate, SVI number) indicating whether these business partners are or are not C-TPAT certified.

For those business partners not eligible for C-TPAT certification, importers must require their business partners to demonstrate that they are meeting C-TPAT security criteria via written/electronic confirmation (e.g., contractual obligations; via a letter from a senior business partner officer attesting to compliance; a written statement from the business partner demonstrating their compliance with C-TPAT security criteria or an equivalent WCO accredited security program administered by a foreign customs authority; or by providing a completed importer security questionnaire). Based upon a documented risk-assessment process, non-CTPAT-eligible business partners must be subject to verification of compliance with C-TPAT security criteria by the importer.

Point of Origin

Importers must ensure that business partners develop security processes and procedures consistent with the C-TPAT security criteria to enhance the integrity of the shipment at point of origin.

Periodic reviews of business partners' processes and facilities should be conducted based on risk and should maintain the security standards required by the importer.

Participation/Certification in Foreign Customs Administrations Supply Chain Security Programs

Current or prospective business partners who have obtained a certification in a supply chain security program being administered by a foreign customs administration should be required to indicate their status of participation to the importer.

OTHER INTERNAL CRITERIA FOR SELECTION

Internal requirements, such as financial soundness, capability of meeting contractual security requirements, and the ability to identify and correct security deficiencies as needed, should be addressed by the importer. Internal requirements should be assessed against a risk-based process as determined by an internal management team.

Container Security

Container integrity must be maintained to protect against the introduction of unauthorized material and/or persons. At point of stuffing, procedures must be in place to properly seal and maintain the integrity of the shipping containers. A high-security seal must be affixed to all loaded containers bound for the United States. All seals must meet or exceed the current PAS ISO 17712 standards for high-security seals.

CONTAINER INSPECTION

Procedures must be in place to verify the physical integrity of the container structure prior to stuffing, to include the reliability of the locking mechanisms of the doors. A seven-point inspection process is recommended for all containers:

- Front wall
- Left side

- Right side
- Floor
- Ceiling/roof
- Inside/outside doors
- Outside/undercarriage

CONTAINER SEALS

Written procedures must stipulate how seals are to be controlled and affixed to loaded containers, to include procedures for recognizing and reporting compromised seals and/or containers to U.S. Customs and Border Protection or the appropriate foreign authority. Only designated employees should distribute container seals for integrity purposes.

CONTAINER STORAGE

Containers must be stored in a secure area to prevent unauthorized access and/or manipulation. Procedures must be in place for reporting and neutralizing unauthorized entry into containers or container storage areas.

Physical Access Controls

Access controls prevent unauthorized entry to facilities, maintain control of employees and visitors, and protect company assets. Access controls must include the positive identification of all employees, visitors, and vendors at all points of entry.

EMPLOYEES

An employee identification system must be in place for positive identification and access control purposes. Employees should be given access only to those secure areas needed for the performance of their duties. Company management or security personnel must adequately control the issuance and removal of employee, visitor, and vendor identification badges.

Procedures for the issuance, removal, and changing of access devices (e.g., keys or key cards) must be documented.

VISITORS

Visitors must present photo identification for documentation purposes upon arrival. All visitors should be escorted and visibly display temporary identification.

DELIVERIES (INCLUDING MAIL)

Proper vendor ID and/or photo identification must be presented for documentation purposes upon arrival by all vendors. Arriving packages and mail should be periodically screened before being disseminated.

CHALLENGING AND REMOVING UNAUTHORIZED PERSONS

Procedures must be in place to identify, challenge, and address unauthorized or unidentified persons.

Personnel Security

Processes must be in place to screen prospective employees and to periodically check current employees.

PREEMPLOYMENT VERIFICATION

Application information, such as employment history and references, must be verified prior to employment.

BACKGROUND CHECKS AND INVESTIGATIONS

Consistent with foreign, federal, state, and local regulations, background checks and investigations should be conducted for prospective employees. Once employed, periodic checks and reinvestigations should be performed based on cause and/or the sensitivity of the employee's position.

PERSONNEL TERMINATION PROCEDURES

Companies must have procedures in place to remove identification, facility, and system access for terminated employees.

PROCEDURAL SECURITY

Security measures must be in place to ensure the integrity and security of processes relevant to the transportation, handling, and storage of cargo in the supply chain.

DOCUMENTATION PROCESSING

Procedures must be in place to ensure that all information used in the clearing of merchandise/cargo is legible, complete, accurate, and protected against the exchange, loss, or introduction of erroneous information. Documentation control must include safeguarding computer access and information.

Manifesting Procedures

To help ensure the integrity of cargo received from abroad, procedures must be in place to ensure that information received from business partners is reported accurately and timely.

Shipping and Receiving

Arriving cargo should be reconciled against information on the cargo manifest. The cargo should be accurately described and the weights, labels, marks, and piece count indicated and verified.

Departing cargo should be verified against purchase or delivery orders. Drivers delivering or receiving cargo must be positively identified before cargo is received or released.

CARGO DISCREPANCIES

All shortages, overages, and other significant discrepancies or anomalies must be resolved and/or investigated appropriately. Customs and/or other appropriate law enforcement agencies must be notified if illegal or suspicious activities are detected—as appropriate.

Security Training and Threat Awareness

A threat awareness program should be established and maintained by security personnel to recognize and foster awareness of the threat posed by terrorists at each point in the supply chain.

Employees must be made aware of the procedures the company has in place to address a situation and how to report it. Additional training should be provided to employees in the shipping and receiving areas, as well as those receiving and opening mail.

Additionally, specific training should be offered to assist employees in maintaining cargo integrity, recognizing internal conspiracies, and protecting access controls. These programs should offer incentives for active employee participation.

Physical Security

Cargo handling and storage facilities in domestic and foreign locations must have physical barriers and deterrents that guard against unauthorized access. Importers should incorporate the following C-TPAT physical security criteria throughout their supply chains as applicable.

FENCING

Perimeter fencing should enclose the areas around cargo handling and storage facilities. Interior fencing within a cargo handling structure should be used to segregate domestic, international, high value, and hazardous cargo. All fencing must be regularly inspected for integrity and damage.

GATES AND GATEHOUSES

Gates through which vehicles and/or personnel enter or exit must be manned and/or monitored. The number of gates should be kept to the minimum necessary for proper access and safety.

PARKING

Private passenger vehicles should be prohibited from parking in or adjacent to cargo handling and storage areas.

BUILDING STRUCTURE

Buildings must be constructed of materials that resist unlawful entry. The integrity of structures must be maintained by periodic inspection and repair.

LOCKING DEVICES AND KEY CONTROLS

All external and internal windows, gates, and fences must be secured with locking devices. Management or security personnel must control the issuance of all locks and keys.

LIGHTING

Adequate lighting must be provided inside and outside the facility, including the following areas: entrances and exits, cargo handling and storage areas, fence lines, and parking areas.

ALARM SYSTEMS AND VIDEO SURVEILLANCE CAMERAS

Alarm systems and video surveillance cameras should be utilized to monitor premises and prevent unauthorized access to cargo handling and storage areas.

Information Technology Security

PASSWORD PROTECTION

Automated systems must use individually assigned accounts that require a periodic change of password. IT security policies, procedures, and standards must be in place and provided to employees in the form of training.

ACCOUNTABILITY

A system must be in place to identify the abuse of IT, including improper access, tampering, or the altering of business data. All system violators must be subject to appropriate disciplinary actions for abuse.

Appendix B. C-TPAT Exporter Requirements

Since its inception, the Customs-Trade Partnership against Terrorism (C-TPAT) program has sought to enhance supply chain security throughout the international supply chain, from point of stuffing through to the first U.S. port of arrival. As the C-TPAT program has continued its evolution, it has become apparent that exports also have an important role in international supply chains, and while this sector is not as heavily owned by U.S. Customs and Border Protection (CBP) and the C-TPAT program, developing an export component for C-TPAT would further enhance both the program and its relationship with other mutually recognized foreign customs administrations.

Definition

For C-TPAT purposes, an exporter is defined as a person or company who, as the principal party in interest in the export transaction, has the power and responsibility for determining and controlling the sending of the items out of the United States.

Exporter Entity Eligibility Requirements

Entities that wish to participate in the C-TPAT exporter program must meet with the program's definition of an exporter as well as meet with the following eligibility requirements:

1. Be an active U.S. exporter out of the United States.
2. Have a business office staffed in the United States.
3. Be an active U.S. exporter with a documentable
    a. Employee Identification Number (EIN) or
    b. Dun & Bradstreet (DUNS) number.
4. Have a documented export security program and a designated officer or manager who will act as the C-TPAT program main point of contact. Additionally, the participant should have an alternate point of contact should the designated point of contact be unavailable.

5. Commit to maintaining the C-TPAT supply chain security criteria as outlined in the C-TPAT exporter agreement.
6. Create and provide CBP with a C-TPAT supply chain security profile which identifies how the exporter will meet, maintain, and enhance internal policy to meet the C-TPAT exporter security criteria.
7. In order to be eligible, the exporter must have an acceptable level of compliance for export reporting for the latest 12-month period and be in good standing with U.S. regulatory bodies, such as the Department of Commerce, Department of State, Department of Treasury, Nuclear Regulatory Commission, Drug Enforcement Administration, and Department of Defense.

Exporter Minimum Security Criteria

C-TPAT recognizes the complexity of international supply chains and endorses the application and implementation of security measures based upon risk analysis by exporters. Therefore, the program allows for flexibility and the customization of security plans based on the member's business model. Appropriate security measures, as listed throughout this document, must be implemented and maintained throughout the above C-TPAT export participants' supply chains. Exporters must conduct a comprehensive risk assessment of their international supply chain based upon the following C-TPAT security criteria. Where an exporter outsources or contracts elements of its supply chain, such as to a warehouse, logistics provider, carrier, or other export supply chain element, the exporter must work with these business partners to ensure that effective security measures are in place and adhered to throughout the entire supply chain.

Business Partner Requirements

Exporters must have written and verifiable processes for the screening and selection of business partners, including service providers, manufacturers, product suppliers, and vendors. Where applicable, these processes must include checks against the Department of Commerce/Bureau of Industry and Security (BIS), Department of State/Directorate of Defense Trade Controls (DDTC), and Department of Treasury/Office of Foreign Assets Control (OFAC) lists. Entities on prohibited lists should be reported to the SCSS and relevant authority within 24 hours prior to departure.

Security Procedures

Written procedures must exist for screening business partners that identify specific factors or practices the presence of which would trigger additional scrutiny by the exporter.

For those business partners eligible for C-TPAT certification (importers, carriers, ports, terminals, brokers, consolidators, etc.), the exporter must have documentation (e.g., SVI number) indicating whether these business partners are or are not C-TPAT certified and/or participating in a reciprocal Authorized Economic Operator (AEO) program (e.g., AEO certificate).

For those business partners not eligible for C-TPAT certification or participation in an AEO program, exporters must require their business partners to demonstrate that they are meeting C-TPAT security criteria via written/electronic confirmation (e.g., contractual obligations; via a letter from a senior business partner officer attesting to compliance; a written statement from the business partner demonstrating their compliance with C-TPAT security criteria or an equivalent AEO security program administered by a foreign customs authority; or by providing a completed exporter security questionnaire). Based upon a documented risk-assessment process, non-CTPAT-eligible business partners must be subject to verification of compliance with C-TPAT security criteria by the exporter.

Risk assessments of the company's export program must be completed on an annual basis.

Point of Origin

Exporters must inform business partners of security processes and procedures that are consistent with the C-TPAT security criteria to enhance the integrity of the shipment at point of export.

Periodic reviews of business partners' processes and facilities should be conducted based on risk to maintain the security standards required by the exporter.

PARTICIPATION/CERTIFICATION IN FOREIGN CUSTOMS ADMINISTRATIONS' SUPPLY CHAIN SECURITY PROGRAMS

Current or prospective business partners who have obtained a certification in a supply chain security program being administered by a foreign customs administration should be required to indicate their status of participation to the exporter.

OTHER INTERNAL CRITERIA FOR SELECTION

Internal requirements, such as financial soundness, capability of meeting contractual security requirements, and the ability to identify and correct security deficiencies as needed, should be addressed by the exporter. Internal requirements should be assessed by management utilizing a risk-based document.

Container Security

Container integrity must be maintained to protect against the introduction of unauthorized material and/or persons. At point of stuffing, written procedures must be in place to properly seal and maintain the integrity of the shipping containers.

CONTAINER INSPECTION

Procedures must be in place to verify the physical integrity of the container structure prior to stuffing, to include the reliability of the locking mechanisms of the doors. A seven-point inspection process is recommended for all containers:

- Front wall
- Left side
- Right side
- Floor
- Ceiling/roof
- Inside/outside doors, door hardware, and fasteners
- Outside/undercarriage

CONTAINER SEALS

The sealing of export containers, to include continuous seal integrity, is a crucial element of a secure supply chain and remains a critical part of an exporter's commitment to C-TPAT. A high-security seal must be affixed to all loaded containers destined for export from the United States.

All seals must meet or exceed the current ISO 17712 standards for high-security seals.

Written procedures must stipulate how seals are to be controlled and affixed to loaded export containers, to include procedures for recognizing and reporting compromised seals and/or containers to CBP or the appropriate foreign authority.

Only designated employees should distribute seals for integrity purposes.

CONTAINER STORAGE

Containers must be stored in a secure area to prevent unauthorized access and/or manipulation and to ensure container integrity is being maintained, especially to protect against the introduction of unauthorized material.

Procedures must be in place for reporting and neutralizing unauthorized entry into containers or container storage areas and any structural changes, such as a hidden compartment, discovered in containers destined for export. Notification should be made within 24 hours of discovery to the assigned supply chain security specialist (SCSS).

Conveyance Tracking and Monitoring Procedures

Exporters should ensure that their transportation providers adhere to the following tracking and monitoring procedures:

- Conveyance and container integrity should be maintained while the conveyance is en route transporting cargo to the point of export. Utilizing a tracking and monitoring activity log or equivalent technology is required. If driver logs are utilized, they should reflect that trailer/container integrity was verified.
- Predetermined routes should be identified by the transportation provider for the exporter, and these procedures should consist of random route checks by the transportation provider along with documenting and verifying the length of time between the loading point/trailer pickup, the export point, and/or the delivery destinations, during peak and nonpeak times.
- Drivers should notify the dispatcher of any route delays due to weather, traffic, and/or rerouting.
- Transportation provider management must perform a documented, periodic, and unannounced verification process to ensure the logs are maintained and conveyance tracking and monitoring procedures are being followed and enforced.
- Drivers must report and should document any anomalies or unusual structural modifications found on the conveyance or container.

Physical Access Controls

Access controls prevent unauthorized entry to cargo facilities, maintain control of employees and visitors, and protect company assets. Access controls must include the positive identification of all employees, visitors, service providers, and vendors at all points of entry. Employees and service providers should have access only to those areas of a facility where they have legitimate *business.*

EMPLOYEES

An employee identification system must be in place for positive identification and access control purposes. Employees should be given access only to those secure areas needed for the performance of their duties. Company management or security personnel must adequately control the issuance and removal of employee, visitor, and vendor identification badges.

Procedures for the issuance, removal and changing of access devices (e.g. keys, key cards, etc.) must be documented.

VISITORS/VENDORS/SERVICE PROVIDERS

Visitors must present photo identification for documentation purposes upon arrival. All visitors should be escorted and provided temporary identification that must be visibly displayed on their person.

CHALLENGING AND REMOVING UNAUTHORIZED PERSONS

Procedures must be in place to identify, challenge, and address unauthorized or unidentified persons.

DELIVERIES (INCLUDING MAIL)

Proper ID and/or photo identification must be presented for documentation purposes upon arrival by transportation providers. Arriving packages and mail should be periodically screened before being disseminated.

Personnel Security

Processes must be in place to screen prospective employees and to periodically check current employees.

PREEMPLOYMENT VERIFICATION

Application information, such as employment history and references, must be verified prior to employment.

BACKGROUND CHECKS AND INVESTIGATIONS

Consistent with, federal, state, and local regulations, background checks and investigations should be conducted for prospective employees. Once employed, periodic checks and reinvestigations should be performed based on cause and/or the sensitivity of the employee's position.

PERSONNEL TERMINATION PROCEDURES

Companies must have procedures in place to remove identification, facility, and system access for terminated employees.

Procedural Security

Security measures must be in place to ensure the integrity and security of processes relevant to the transportation, handling, and storage of cargo in the supply chain.

Security procedures should be implemented that restrict access to the export shipment. The procedures should prevent the lading of contraband while en route from facilities in domestic locations prior to export from the United States.

CARGO DISCREPANCIES

All shortages, overages, and other significant discrepancies or anomalies must be resolved and or investigated appropriately.

Customs, the assigned supply chain security specialist, and/or other appropriate law enforcement agencies must be notified if illegal or suspicious activities are detected as appropriate.

DOCUMENTATION PROCESSING

Procedures must be in place to ensure that all information used in the preparation of merchandise/cargo for export (EEI or other required export form) is legible, complete, accurate, and protected against the exchange, loss, or introduction of erroneous information. Documentation control must include safeguarding computer access and information.

BILL OF LADING/AIRWAY BILL/MANIFESTING PROCEDURES

To help ensure the integrity of cargo being exported, procedures must be in place to ensure that information transmitted/received to/from business partners is reported accurately and timely.

SHIPPING

The export cargo should be accurately described and the weights, labels, marks, and piece count indicated and verified. Departing cargo should be verified against purchase or delivery orders. Drivers delivering or receiving cargo must be positively identified before cargo is received or released.

SCREENING FOR PROHIBITED OR RESTRICTED PARTIES

Documentable procedures and processes must exist to identify any party on lists from State/DDTC, Commerce/BIS, or Treasury/OFAC denied persons and who are involved in an export transaction with the exporter. Entities on prohibited lists should be reported to the SCSS and relevant authority within 24 hours prior to departure.

Physical Security

Procedures must be in place to prevent, detect, or deter undocumented material and unauthorized personnel from gaining access to conveyance, including concealment in containers.

Cargo handling and storage facilities in domestic locations should have physical barriers and deterrents that guard against unauthorized access. Exporters should, according to their business models, incorporate the following C-TPAT physical security criteria throughout their supply chains as practical and appropriate.

FENCING

Perimeter fencing should enclose the areas around cargo handling and storage facilities. Interior fencing within a cargo handling structure should be used to segregate domestic, international, high value, and hazardous cargo. All fencing must be regularly inspected for integrity and damage.

GATES AND GATEHOUSES

Gates through which vehicles and/or personnel enter or exit must be manned and/or monitored. The number of gates should be kept to the minimum necessary for proper access and safety.

PARKING

Private passenger vehicles should be prohibited from parking in or adjacent to cargo handling and storage areas.

BUILDING STRUCTURE

Buildings must be constructed of materials that resist unlawful entry. The integrity of structures must be maintained by periodic inspection and repair.

LOCKING DEVICES AND KEY CONTROLS

All external and internal windows, gates, and fences must be secured with locking devices. Management or security personnel must control the issuance of all locks and keys.

LIGHTING

Adequate lighting must be provided inside and outside the facility, including the following areas: entrances and exits, cargo handling and storage areas, fence lines, and parking areas.

ALARM SYSTEMS AND VIDEO SURVEILLANCE CAMERAS

Alarm systems and video surveillance cameras should be utilized to monitor premises and prevent unauthorized access to cargo handling and storage areas.

Export Training and Threat Awareness

A C-TPAT exporter must have a documented export security program as well as a designated officer or manager who will act as the C-TPAT program point of contact. This program should have support throughout the corporate structure of the company displayed in correspondence to personnel.

A threat awareness program should be established and maintained to recognize and foster awareness of the threat posed by illegal activities at each point in the supply chain, to include final point of export. There should be documented procedures on how the export security officer or manager receives information about changes in regulations or procedures.

Employees must be made aware of the procedures the company has in place to address a security incident or suspicion thereof and how to report it.

Additional training should be provided to employees in vital export areas, such as the shipping and receiving areas, as well as those receiving and opening mail.

Additionally, specific training should be offered to assist employees in maintaining cargo integrity, recognizing internal conspiracies, protecting access controls, and enhancing physical security.

These programs should offer incentives for active employee participation.

Information Technology Security

PASSWORD PROTECTION

Automated systems must use individually assigned accounts that require a periodic change of password. IT security policies, procedures, and standards must be in place and provided to employees in the form of training.

ACCOUNTABILITY

A system must be in place to identify the abuse of IT, including improper access, tampering, or the altering of business data. All system violators must be subject to appropriate disciplinary actions for abuse.

About the Author

Kati Suominen is an adjunct fellow with the CSIS Europe Program; the founder and CEO of both the equity crowd-funding platform TradeUp Capital Fund and the trade research and platform firm Nextrade Group, LLC; and an adjunct professor at the Anderson School of Management at the University of California–Los Angeles. She previously served as a fellow at the German Marshall Fund and as trade economist at the Inter-American Development Bank. She has authored over 80 articles and 9 books on trade and is now working on her 10th, *Globalization 4.0: How Disruptive Technologies Revolutionize Economies and Clash with Policy in the Hyperconnected World*. She has provided commentary in the *Wall Street Journal*, Bloomberg, BBC, CSPAN, CNN, *Washington Post*, *Los Angeles Times*, *Politico*, *USA Today*, *Time*, Economist Intelligence Unit, and *U.S. News and World Report*, among others. Dr. Suominen is a pioneer in global digital economy policies and e-commerce issues. She also has deep expertise in trade and economic integration, chairs a global expert group on regional trade agreements for the International Center for Trade and Sustainable Development and the World Economic Forum, and she is the idea woman of RTAExchange.org, a new forum on trade agreements. A graduate of the University of Pennsylvania's Wharton School (MBA) and the University of California–San Diego (PhD), she is a life member of the Council on Foreign Relations and an American Assembly's Next Generation Fellow. She serves on the advisory boards of trade-related groups GlobeTrade.com, New Markets Lab, and Women Entrepreneurs Grow Global, and National Law Center for Inter-American Free Trade.

www.ingramcontent.com/pod-product-compliance
Ingram Content Group UK Ltd.
Pitfield, Milton Keynes, MK11 3LW, UK
UKHW051418150926
475561UK00005B/227

9 781442 240902